GLOBETROT KT-482-993

Travel Guide

NEW YORK CITY

MICHAEL LEECH

NEW HOLLAND

NEW
HOLLAND

★★★ Highly recommended
★★ Recommended
★ See if you can

Sixth edition published in 2009
by New Holland Publishers (UK) Ltd
London • Cape Town • Sydney • Auckland
10 9 8 7 6 5 4 3 2 1
website: www.newhollandpublishers.com

Garfield House, 86 Edgware Road, London,
W2 2EA, United Kingdom

80 McKenzie Street, Cape Town,
8001, South Africa

Unit 1, 66 Gibbes Street
Chatswood NSW 2067 Australia

218 Lake Road, Northcote
Auckland, New Zealand

Distributed in the USA by
The Globe Pequot Press, Connecticut

ISBN 978 1 84773 384 9

Publishing Manager: Thea Grobbelaar
DTP Cartographic Manager: Genené Hart
Editors: Carla Zietsman, Nicky Steenkamp,
Melany McCallum, Susannah Coucher
Cartographers: Rudi de Lange, Tanja Spinola,
Renée Barnes
Design and DTP: Nicole Bannister, Sonya Cupido
Picture Researchers: Shavonne Govender, Jan Croot
Consultant: Christopher Rice

Reproduction by Hirt & Carter (Pty) Ltd, Cape Town
Printed and bound by Times Offset (M) Sdn. Bhd.,
Malaysia.

The author's special thanks go to NYTravel Advisory
Bureau, the press office at NY Convention and Visitors'
Bureau, and Magellan Public Relations, London.

Photographic Credits:
Jon Arnold Images, page 108; The Bridgeman Art
Library/Frick Collection, New York, page 87; The Chelsea
Hotel, page 62; Chris Warren Picture Library, page 112,
64; Christine Osborne Pictures, pages 25 (bottom), 28,
43 (top), 44, 46, 47 (top and bottom), 61 (bottom); Thea
Grobbelaar, page 37; Hutchison Library (HL), pages 57,
106; HL/Jeremy A. Horner, pages 9 (bottom), 41 (bot-
tom), 45, 54, 55 (top), 56, 90, 94, 97 (bottom), 105, 107;
HL/Leslie Woodward, pages 55 (bottom), 63; HL/Bernard
Régent, page 51; Caroline Jones, pages 15, 33 (top);
jonarnoldimages.com/Walter Bibikow, page 104; Larry
Luxner, page 77; Life File/Andrew Ward, pages 14, 21,
26; The Mansell Collection, pages 10, 11; Picture Bank
Photo Library, page 38; Pictures Colour Library, pages
17, 71; Robert Harding Picture Library (RHPL), pages 13,
16, 20, 25 (top), 30, 48, 68, 70, 80, 92, 99, 100;
RHPL/G. Robert Cundy, page 111; RHPL/Nigel Francis,
pages 24, 27, 35, 58, 72, 74–76, 84, 91; RHPL/Robert
Francis, page 33 (bottom); RHPL/Michael J. Howell, page
79 (bottom); RHPL/David Lomax, page 10; RHPL/Mike
Newton, pages 9 (top), 69, 73, 93; RHPL/Roy Rainford,
page 110; RHPL/W. Rawlings, pages 19 (top), 22, 34, 85;
RHPL/Ellen Rooney, page 29; RHPL/Bill Ross, page 4;
RHPL/J.E. Stevenson, page 109; RHPL/Paul van Riel,
page 23; RHPL/Viscar, page 18; RHPL/A. Waltham,
pages 79 (top), 103; RHPL/Adam Woolfitt, pages 6, 36,
41 (top), 43 (bottom), 52, 53, 67, 78, 82, 86, 88; Neil
Setchfield, cover, title page, page 19 (bottom); Mireille
Vautier, page 83.

This guidebook has been written by independent
authors and updaters. The information therein repre-
sents their impartial opinion, and neither they nor the
publishers accept payment in return for including in
the book or writing more favourable reviews of any
of the establishments. Whilst every effort has been
made to ensure that this guidebook is as accurate
and up to date as possible, please be aware that the
facts quoted are subject to change, particularly the
price of food, transport and accommodation. The
Publisher accepts no responsibility or liability for any
loss, injury or inconvenience incurred by readers or
travellers using this guide.

Keep us Current
Information in travel guides is apt to change, which is
why we regularly update our guides. We'd be grateful
to receive feedback if you've noted something we
should include in our updates. If you have new
information, please share it with us by writing to the
Publishing Manager, Globetrotter, at the office nearest
to you (addresses on this page). The most significant
contribution to each new edition will receive a free
copy of the updated guide.

Title page: *The Brooklyn Bridge, Lower Manhattan.*
Cover: *Yellow taxis in the streets of New York City.*

CONTENTS

1. **Introducing New York City** 5
   The Land 6
   History in Brief 11
   Government & Economy 18
   The People 20

2. **Lower Manhattan** 31
   The Best of Lower Manhattan 32
   Other Museums and Places of Interest 34
   The Civic Center and South Street Seaport 36

3. **Lower East Side and East Village** 39
   Lower East Side 40
   East Village 45

4. **Greenwich Village, SoHo and TriBeCa** 49
   Greenwich Village 50
   SoHo 54
   TriBeCa 56

5. **Chelsea and Gramercy Park** 59
   Sights to See 60
   Old Residential Districts 62

6. **Midtown** 65
   The Garment District 66
   Shopping Along West 34th Street 68
   Murray Hill and East 42nd Street 70
   Fifth Avenue – West Side 73
   Fifth Avenue – East Side 78

7. **Upper East Side** 81
   Central Park 82
   Museums 84

8. **Upper West Side** 89
   Cultural Venues 90
   Walking on the West Side 92

9. **Harlem and Washington Heights** 95
   Around 125th Street 96
   Washington Heights 98

10. **Beyond Manhattan** 101
    Brooklyn and Queens 102
    The Bronx and Staten Island 104
    Long Island 106
    Beaches 107
    New Jersey 108
    Connecticut 110
    Lower New York State 111

New York City At a Glance 113

Travel Tips 122

Index 127

1
Introducing
New York City

New York is one of those towns that must be seen by sophisticated travellers. Smart, sharp and sweet, New York is always fascinating. This very exciting city incorporates both the best and liveliest of the American Experience and is always awake. For the dedicated nightbird there's no place like **Manhattan**; equally, for those not intrigued by nightclubs, cabarets or bizarre theatrical events, there is an enormous variety of things to do by day. It's the ultimate urban experience: a place to set the heart and senses racing.

New York City isn't simple: it's composed of five boroughs but most visitors venture no further than mighty Manhattan. But consider visits to **Brooklyn**, **Queens**, even the **Bronx**, which has a fantastic botanical garden. A ferry ride over the Hudson to **Staten Island** (actually the fifth borough of Richmond) is one of those great experiences as you take in the **Statue of Liberty**, welcoming you to her towered city on the waves. Unofficially New York also incorporates chunks of nearby New York, the city's suburbs in New York State (one of the biggest in the union) and what you might call NYC country: the rural stretches of northern **New Jersey** and **Long Island**. New Yorkers migrate en masse to small towns and beach resorts in the high heat of summer, transforming places like Easthampton, Fire Island and Amagansett into the city in the country.

Although not a capital, New York has attracted many to its social meltdown. It's a wonderful mixture, and for the sophisticated New Yorker there is just no place like it.

Opposite: *A seagull's view of the business heart of Manhattan.*

Above: *An inkling of how Manhattan used to be can be gained from its major public parks.*
Opposite: *Construction is ever a facet of New York City and jack hammers and steam vents add to the hubbub.*

THE LAND

Three hundred years ago Manhattan was merely a rocky platform above a well-protected harbour opening to the East River and the Hudson. The water-ways are still there but Manhattan has totally changed. To begin with, it has been flattened out and most of its hills removed. To gain an impression of the original geography of the island, walk through **Central Park**, where in parts there is still a certain natural 'feel' of age-old land. Despite the park's overall design with modern paths and roads, huge rocks still thrust up through the terrain, and many of the trees (such as maple) and plants are indigenous.

The rocky foundation of the island meant secure footings for big buildings, and now Manhattan is crowned with the modern equivalent of medieval castles, an impressive and rightly famous parade of steel, glass and concrete towers. The renowned skyline is a riveting sight, especially when you consider that a few decades ago there would have been no tall buildings at all. Major upward expansion began early in the 20th century and has been pushing up vertically ever since. New York's buildings created a new word for a world that, except for Gothic cathedrals, had been up to that time low-rise: skyscraper. Asia now challenges for 'world's tallest buildings' yet New York still has some of the most dramatic constructions the world has ever seen.

The Island Between the Rivers

The rivers to the east and west of Manhattan are natural dividing lines. The **Hudson River** marks the border of New York City and is also the state line between New Jersey and New York. Even so, these settlements are really suburbs of New York that happen to be in another state.

The **East River**, a short waterway from harbour to sea, essentially an inlet with Long Island as its eastern shore, divides Manhattan from Brooklyn and Queens, while the harbour into

NEW YORK CITY	J	F	M	A	M	J	J	A	S	O	N	D
AVERAGE TEMP. °C	0	1	5	11	17	22	25	24	20	15	8	2
AVERAGE TEMP. °F	32	33	41	52	62	71	77	75	68	58	47	36
Days of rainfall	12	10	12	11	11	10	12	10	9	9	9	10
RAINFALL mm	94	97	91	81	81	84	107	109	86	89	76	91
RAINFALL in	4	4	4	3.5	3.5	3.5	4	4	3.5	3.5	3	4

which both rivers feed is the division for Staten Island. The East River also forms the narrow channel between Manhattan and the Bronx, becoming the **Harlem River** running off the Hudson. Every effort has been made to clean up the Harlem River but it is an on-going problem.

Climate

The city essentially has two climates: hot and cold. It's snowy, windy and very cold and frosty in winter, but with a dry, healthy chill that makes for brisk walks and skating in Central Park or in the Rockefeller Center rink. In the sweaty humidity of high summer everyone retreats to air-conditioned offices and apartments if possible. Between these two extremes are brief cool periods of spring and the fall, or autumn, which is often characterized with lovely, warm days and clear skies. New York skies are often cloudless and a brilliant blue.

Plant Life

Some of the city streets are tree-lined, especially in residential areas, and trees and shrubs have benefited from air clean up of lead-free gas and catalytic converters. Many residents fill window sills and flat roofs with tubs and pots. It is certainly worth a trip out to Brooklyn in order to see the specialist collections. Or take a trip to the Bronx for the **New York Botanical Garden** with native plants and the **Bronx Zoo**, but plan a day each for these: they are large and entrances are not close.

THE HUDSON RIVER

The Hudson is a beautiful river, starting in the **Adirondack Mountains**. At its southern end it widens and is the border between NY State and New Jersey. Early residents recall the Hudson as being full of fish, and a great occasion was the annual run of the shad, with the delicious shad roe a popular dish in spring. The valley has varied scenery and historic mansions to explore on day trips by road, rail or NY Waterway.

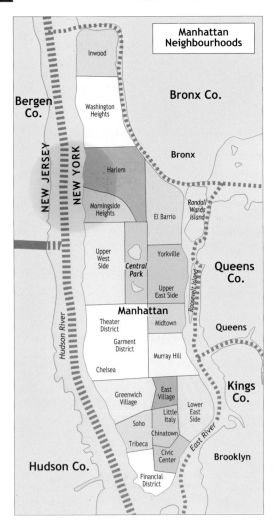

Manhattan Neighbourhoods

Inwood

Bergen Co.

Washington Heights

NEW JERSEY

NEW YORK

Bronx Co.

Bronx

Harlem

Morningside Heights

El Barrio

Randall Wards Island

Upper West Side

Central Park

Yorkville

Upper East Side

Queens Co.

Roosevelt Island

Hudson River

Manhattan

Theater District

Midtown

Queens

Garment District

Murray Hill

Chelsea

Greenwich Village

East Village

Little Italy

Lower East Side

Kings Co.

Soho

Chinatown

Tribeca

Civic Center

Brooklyn

East River

Hudson Co.

Financial District

Wildlife

Even in the concrete city there is a concern for wildlife. Nest boxes are fixed to office walls for peregrine falcons (they prey on the pigeons, which are pests). Central Park contains rare plants, trees and flowers and in the International Wildlife Conservation Center, you will see some 764 species in their habitats.

City Profile

The forming of five boroughs of such disparate size and style appears to have been fairly arbitrary. New York seems to have just grown, without much planning, to what it is now, and is still changing constantly. Yet that is a vital part of what the city is all about and New Yorkers are quite used to roads being dug up, sidewalks cut off, and whole sections being rebuilt. Buildings are replaced almost as quickly, sometimes with ugly 'egg boxes', but often with creations of surprising style. However, you can still find elements of old New York if you search, and it's a rewarding aspect in this ever-modernizing city to find here and there evocative little left-behind bits of another age.

New York originated at its southern tip with the first buildings erected by Dutch settlers in the early 17th century. None of these Colonial buildings exist now but the pattern of streets still shows us what went before: the reason Broadway angles so conspicuously across the island is because originally it was an ancient Indian track.

Contemporary streetplans indicate a settlement which slowly began to develop in the 18th and 19th centuries until in 1811 the Randel Plan was put into effect, mapping out future development of the island according to a **grid system**, with long avenues going north and crossing with narrower east–west streets. This plan goes from 14th Street. Broadway angles right across it; the Financial District is narrower; Greenwich Village streets can puzzle.

Starting in the south, explore the **Battery** and the harbour front. An area which was once renowned for its rowdiness, it is now an international business district and the city's **financial** and **government** **centre**. **Wall Street's** name comes from the first years of the city when it was the street next to the northernmost stockade wall of the burgeoning village. It was there to keep the Algonquin Indians, and later the British, out.

Above: *The Trump Tower on Fifth Avenue is a slice of glass angled to the street.*
Below: *St Mark's Place is a lively and very real part of the city.*

Above: *It may seem confusing, yet signs are clear, routes direct.*

Pressing close are **SoHo** and **TriBeCa**, renovated areas, and now fashionable places for art galleries and studios, then **Greenwich Village** and **Chelsea** followed by **Midtown** and the theatres of **Broadway**. Department stores and airline offices cluster on this part of **Fifth Avenue**. The green spread of **Central Park** divides the **Upper East** and the **Upper West Sides**; at the northern line of the park **Harlem** begins, then **Washington Heights**.

The **boroughs** beyond grew as Manhattan enlarged and needed more workers: they are typical **sleeper suburbs** (where many New York workers reside) with many small independent (detached and split-level) houses, all part of the larger New York, but it's worth remembering that, before its incorporation as a borough in 1898, **Brooklyn** was a separate and prosperous city. The boroughs are cut up with major highways, often elevated, and with main roads curving off in every direction.

New York is necklaced with fast highways, many bridges and tunnels, and in theory it ought to be easy to get around but traffic jams abound at certain times. The continuous unrelenting pressure of traffic, particularly heavy delivery vehicles, is hard on the streets. In addition, penetrating winter frosts literally break up the avenues, causing large and rather dangerous pot holes in the spring through which the yellow taxi cabs lurch.

HISTORY IN BRIEF
Early Settlers

The history of the city begins with the early explorers, who arrived from the 16th century onwards, but little attempt was made to settle until the **Dutch** established a permanent trading post in 1624 which became known as **Nieuw (New) Amsterdam**. There is an ancient tale about Manhattan being purchased from the Native Indians at a bargain price by Peter Minuit, the Director of the Dutch West Indies Company, in 1626. These original settlers (then called Red Indians) had infiltrated from Asia across the Bering Sea millennia ago, and the **Algonquin** tribes had spread along the east coast of the new continent. They reportedly received strings of beads and some gaudy trinkets worth 60 guilders in exchange for their land rights from the thrifty Netherlanders. Whether it is true or not, the original residents called the land 'Manahatta', an Algonquian word probably meaning 'island of the hills'.

The Dutch set about with typical ingenuity to make the hostile island livable, digging canals, smoothing out hills and filling in the shoreline. They beavered

---

'PEG LEG PETE'

The Dutch provided hard work and direction, and a few colourful characters. Notable was Peter Stuyvesant, drafted in from Holland in 1647 as governor to organize a colony that had become lawless and unruly. A stern Calvinist, he curtailed drinking hours in the taverns and came down heavily on free-thinkers and Quakers. Not surprising then that the settlers, who had had things to themselves until his arrival, resented his rigid rule. They would not have been able to comprehend how 'Peg Leg Pete' (so-called on account of his wooden leg) has become a legend, his name labelling institutions and schools.

Left: *In this contemporary etching you get an idea of the tough, arrogant man who was Peter Stuyvesant.*

NEW YORK PASS

The very useful discount pass issued by the New York Travel Advisory saves you money on entry to over 40 museums and sights, as well as other perks, including shopping bargains. Available for periods of 1–7 days, each adult/child's pass comes with a free 140-page guidebook and maps. Buy online at: www.newyorkpass.com or phone (1) 877 714 1999; alternatively, call in at the Visitors' Center at 1560 Broadway (Times Square).

Opposite: *Yet another building will rise as the wrecker's ball destroys old neighbourhoods.*
Below: *The nation's first president and native son, George Washington.*

away for half a century but New Amsterdam wasn't destined to last as a Dutch settlement. **Britain** was eager to increase her overseas possessions, and in 1664, at a time when the British and Dutch were involved in ferocious trade wars, Charles II gave the colony to his brother, the Duke of York. British warships blockaded New York harbour and took the city without firing a single shot. New Amsterdam was then renamed New York.

New York prospered under British rule. The first newspaper, the *New York Gazette*, was established in 1725; in 1754 Columbia University (then called King's) was founded. With its harbour as a prime possession, trade by sea developed constantly. From small beginnings, by the mid-18th century the city had become a major port, and on the eve of the Revolution it was the second largest city in the colonies with 20,000 citizens.

The city was strategically vital during the **War of Independence** (1776–83) and after various skirmishes with Washington's troops, New York was held by the British for the duration. However, the colonies had eventually won their freedom and the British were forced to concede control of the city.

Although it had kept a low wartime profile, New York was briefly the new nation's capital (1785–90) to be followed by Philadelphia (1790–1800). In 1789 **George Washington** was inaugurated as President of the United States in New York's new Federal Hall. Around this time the city developed an infant financial infrastructure by opening the first bank and a stock exchange, thus laying the foundations for its role as a world financial centre.

The Making of the Metropolis

As Manhattan flowed relentlessly north, hemmed in by its two rivers, it developed a series of defined districts. Inevitably many of these have changed, some beyond all recognition – for this was originally an island of small farms. It may be hard to imagine now, especially as these rural settlements have become the Financial District. The Lower East Side is no longer the same place where waves of 19th-century immigrants settled in overcrowded tenement buildings, and Midtown has few of its original distinctive brownstone row houses.

As the nation's premier seaport in a new, aggressive nation, New York became increasingly wealthy. In 1811 the city governors came up with the **Randel Plan**, a grid system that catered for future expansion by laying out New York in over 2000 rectangular blocks.

Despite the British blockade of New York harbour in the War of 1812, the city continued to prosper. The opening of the **Erie Canal** in 1825 gave the east coast access to trade with the US interior and the Canadian lakes. By the middle of the century, New York was the most prosperous city in the country; traders and industrial tycoons were making fortunes. Manufacturing increased and the rich moved uptown.

POSTAL CODES

If you have been given an address in Manhattan you may not have much idea where it is, even though cross streets are consecutively numbered. Avenues are long and there are some named, not num- bered, roads (for example, Columbus, Amsterdam, Greenwich and Park Avenue, Central Park South and West). The postcode system is simple: addresses in Manhattan have a set of eight digits – ignore the last three: the previous 2 will tell you the district post office's number. Post office maps show the actual areas of each zone. For example: 10036 is Midtown and Theater District; 10011 Greenwich Village–Lower Fifth Avenue; 10028 is Upper East Side.

PROHIBITION

As alcohol was denied under legislation in 1919, so illegal drinking of 'bathtub gin' and other home-made liquors grew and crime prospered in the new lucrative market. Speakeasies (drinking dens) flourished all over New York. It was fashionable for the wealthy to go up to Harlem to the Cotton Club to dance, drink and drug, to hear the new jazz and see the black stars emerging from that vital hotspot. The way that most poor Harlem residents lived was totally unknown to most well-off New Yorkers, but it was smart and life was fast and exhilarating.

Immigration

In the 19th century immigration rolled in like a tide, and New York was the main receiving point for settlers from Europe. The new arrivals came by sea, often after a fearful crossing. Africans were brought in to the southern ports of the United States as slaves. Many moved north to find a free life and in New York they headed for the borough of Harlem.

HISTORICAL CALENDAR

?BC–16th century Land occupied by groups of Algonquin Indians.
1524 Giovanni da Verrazano sails into New York harbour.
1609 Henry Hudson, working for the Dutch, arrives in New York Bay.
1624 The Dutch establish first trading post.
1626 Peter Minuit buys Manhattan for a few trinkets.
1647 Peter Stuyvesant becomes governor.
1664 The British snatch the colony and change its name to New York.
1776 War of Independence begins.
1783 USA wins independence; British evacuate New York.
1785–90 New York is USA capital.
1812–14 British blockade New York harbour.
1825 Erie Canal opens.
1835 Fire razes much of city to ground.
1858 Central Park designed.

1861–5 American Civil War.
1868 First elevated railroad built on Greenwich Street.
1883 Brooklyn Bridge was completed.
1886 Statue of Liberty unveiled.
1892 Cathedral of St John the Divine begun; Ellis Island opens.
1909 Wilbur Wright flies first plane over New York.
1911 Triangle Shirtwaist Factory fire kills 146 sweat-shop workers; New York Public Library completed.
1919 18th Amendment bans alcohol and launches Prohibition.
1929 Stock Market Crash followed by the Great Depression.
1931 Empire State becomes world's tallest building.
1933 Prohibition ends; Fiorello LaGuardia becomes mayor.
1941–45 USA involved in World War II.
1946 UN establishes HQ in

New York.
1948 Idlewild Airport opens. Now JFK.
1954 Ellis Island closes.
1962 Avery Fisher Hall, first building in Lincoln Center, completed.
1973 World Trade Center completed.
1976 Statue of Liberty restored for her 100th year.
1980–90 Near bankruptcy then boom.
1990s 42nd Street clean up.
1994 Mayor Guiliani elected on a clean up New York City programme.
1996 Victory Theater re-opened.
2000 Hilary Clinton elected Senator for NYS.
2001–2008 The World Trade Towers destroyed. Work on the new World Trade Center is due for com-pletion in 2012. Remodeling of Times Square/Broadway continues with new hotels. It's safe, the area blossoms, new theatres open.

Between 1840–57, three million Irish and Germans arrived in New York harbour. Most fanned out across America to create a new nation, though many stayed in the city. New York was unprepared for such an influx: fires, epidemics, overcrowding and fearful poverty ensued. The gap between rich and poor widened; there were riots and looting.

After the Civil War, New York embarked on a grand scale of civic building. Central Park was created in 1858; a range of apartment blocks, hotels and department stores were built and railways – both national and local – were developed. In 1880 the Metropolitan Museum of Art opened; around the same time the New York Public Library and Carnegie Hall were founded. The landmark Brooklyn Bridge was completed in 1883.

From 1870 onwards a new wave of Italian, east European and Chinese immigrants came to New York. Ellis Island opened in 1892 to facilitate their entry. At the turn of the century, the population density of the Lower East Side (where most of the immigrants lived) was 330,000 per sq mile, the highest in the world. Living and working conditions were appalling. Tenement buildings were unhygienic and overcrowded. People toiled long hours for a pittance in dangerous sweatshops. Working conditions didn't improve until after the Triangle

ALGONQUIN ROUND TABLE

Renowned for her smart quips ('you can lead a whore to culture but you cannot make her think'), **Dorothy Parker** was a queen among the wordsharps who met at the Algonquin Hotel, just over the road from the *New Yorker* offices. She and other wits held up a mirror to the times, and gave New York much of the image it preserves today as a centre of smart repartee, humorous verse and quick cracks. Alas, the Algonquin (on West 43rd Street) hasn't resounded with such hilarity for decades, but writers, agents and publishers still meet there and you can visit, have tea or a drink in its foyer, and enjoy its unique clubby atmosphere. You can even dine at the famous Round Table installed for the benefit of Parker and her cohorts.

Opposite: *The Immigration Halls on Ellis Island, where for a century new arrivals were processed, are now a museum.*
Left: *Brooklyn Bridge is a splendid vantage point from which to view the city.*

Shirtwaist Factory fire in 1911, when 146 young women working in a sweatshop were burned to death. Tougher laws and fire escapes were then implemented.

Between the Wars

The United States played a considerable part in the realigning of Europe when wartime chaos ended in 1918. It then entered into a frenetic time of expansion and money-making in the 1920s. This was reflected mostly in the big cities which became like magnets to anyone who wanted to feel they were in the centre of things. The biggest magnet of all was New York.

Picture files of the period bulge with shots of the fashionable and famous descending from ocean liners along the Hudson River Docks. Film stars, fashion designers, fast-living aristocrats and the new business tycoons, as well as famous names from Noël Coward to Gertrude Stein, arrived and were swept up by the excitement. The theatre boomed, although the fledgling film industry had already moved to California, where the sun was more certain. Skyscrapers rocketed up; foundations were laid for the Chrysler Building, the Empire State and the Rockefeller Center.

The 1920s were a time of growth and high living, epitomized by New York's flamboyant mayor, Jimmy Walker. Alcohol was outlawed but speakeasies flourished. The economic boom began to spiral out of control and confidence in the stock market came to an abrupt end with the Wall Street Crash in October 1929. By 1932 Walker had resigned amid accusations of corruption. More than a quarter of New Yorkers were out of work and thousands lived in shantytowns known as 'Hoovervilles'

Below: *Soaring up against summer skies, the Chrysler was the tallest building in the world for about a year.*

Left: *An impressive parade of the flags of the members represented at the United Nations.*

(after the president). The USA was in the grip of the terrible **Great Depression**. This continued right up until the mid-1930s and was only alleviated by radical government intervention. In New York the WPA or Works Progress Administration was greatly responsible for the city's economic recovery, creating thousands of jobs and encouraging projects from construction to artworks.

Post-War New York

A new mood prevailed after 1945 and the accent was on growth again. The United Nations established its headquarters here in 1946, a major coup for the city. Idlewild Airport (renamed John F. Kennedy Airport after the president's assasination in 1963) was opened in 1948 to encourage more business. Like the alternative Newark Airport, it has fast connections to Manhattan. The huge flood of immigrants had greatly slowed down so in 1954 Ellis Island processed its last New American. It is now a museum. New buildings include the Lever Building, the Seagram and the Lincoln Center. The Financial District was rebuilt though its World Trade Towers were 25 years old when felled in 2001.

Recent decades witnessed racial strife, crime and violence, now under control, making NYC one of USA's safest places. The city has gone through financial crises but had solid growth since the '90s. It's a regenerated positive city, but still with a notable 'rich/poor' divide.

THE WALL STREET CRASH

Although there had been warnings and tremors, the Crash was not expected and everyone was encouraged to gamble. Huge sums were being made on the Stock Market and this paved the way for a dreadful and shocking fall in October 1929 that paralyzed not only the United States but the whole world. It resulted in the Depression and New Yorkers suffered as much as the rest of the country. Strangely enough, there was some growth during this period – such as civil projects which included the construction of the city's skyscrapers and Rockefeller Center. An ever-changing city, it continues to tear down and re-erect new ones.

GOVERNMENT AND ECONOMY

The Mayor of New York is no mere figurehead: he (or maybe one day she) is a very powerful political force, as epitomized by Mayor Fiorello LaGuardia or, more recently, Rudolph Giuliani. In 1989 New York's government was reformed and now it is a 35-member city council. Each of the five boroughs has a certain amount of independence of legislation.

New York has always been a boom-and-bust town, and it continues to lurch from crisis to crisis in government, with few people believing in the evergreen promises of politicians. Things came to a head in the 1970s after a period of unrest in the previous decade, when riots were witnessed in Harlem after the terrible assassinations of the era, notably of President Kennedy and the Reverend Martin Luther King.

In the mid-1970s came the announcement that New York was virtually bankrupt. Mayor Ed Koch's emergency measures revived business and construction, but a period of uncertainty followed the First Gulf War and the recession of the early 1990s. Koch's replacement, New York's first black mayor, David Dinkins, elected on a platform of continuing growth, moved over for Rudy Giuliani in 1992. His zero-tolerance policy dramatically reduced crime rates in the city. New York's current mayor, Michael Bloomberg (last re-elected in 2005) aims to balance the budget, reduce unemployment to a record low and combat poverty.

Although poverty and crime are still very evident in some quarters, with the lack of jobs being a major problem particularly for disadvantaged youth, somehow the city manages to pull through. New Yorkers are a tough breed, and they love their city, warts and all. They continue to support the dream that there is such a state as a healthy and financially balanced city, beliefs which instill strength and confidence in the populace. As its citizens go on, so does New York.

MANHATTAN FACT FILE

Population: 7.4 million.
Area: 13.4 miles (21.5km) long; 2.3 miles (3.7km) wide.
Taxis: 12,000.
Art galleries: there are about 500 galleries.
Skyscrapers: there are about 200 skyscrapers.
Broadway theatres: there are 40 recognized Broadway theatres.
Lower Manhattan: 30% is built on reclaimed land created by landfills.
Empire State Building: visibility from the 102nd floor on a clear day is an amazing 80 miles (129km). Celebrated its 75th birthday in 2006.
'Big Apple': a term coined in the 1920s by jazz musicians as a way of saying 'There are many apples on the tree, but when you pick New York City, you pick the Big Apple.'

Economic Development

A fact that makes many non-New Yorkers envious is that New York is first in so many fields. The number one city in the United States, it is also the biggest conference and incentive meeting place in the country. It's the major **business** and **financial** centre, with the number one stock exchanges. Although trade by sea has fallen away, it still acts as a major port and its three airports handle cargoes from around the world. **Industry** is a giant and there's a big construction business, and constant encouraging of new companies to come and set up, particularly in the outer boroughs beyond Manhattan. **Fashion** and the garment industry are big employers. **Tourism** is a major money-winner bringing billions to the city each year. As such, the city has developed both the infrastructure and the attractions, making it the most exciting visitor destination in the world. The theatre and **entertainment** industries, volatile though they are, flourish and encourage a whole growth of other industries from taxi services and parking lots to hotels and restaurants. The **arts** are big money here – major auction houses flourish and there is more book-publishing than anywhere else in the country.

Above: *Street signs plaster poles on the corners and they can be confusing.*

FIFTH AVENUE

A name that still resounds with glamour, this long avenue goes all the way from the **Washington Arch** below 8th Street to 125th Street in Harlem. It gives a view of the city as it changes dramatically, from the casual air of **Greenwich Village** to smart **Midtown**. An almost country-like stretch edges the park in the wealthy **Upper East Side** to a rundown end beyond 110th Street in **Spanish Harlem**. It is the spine of the city, dividing East and West. Many famous buildings stand along it.

Opposite: *President Kennedy was not a New Yorker but he and his wife maintained a residence here, as do President and Mrs Clinton.*
Left: *Shopping on Fifth Avenue is a delight.*

NEW YORK HUMOUR

Like all great cities, from London to Berlin and Paris to Sydney, New York has its own decided sense of humour. It probably started with the immigrants, who had to be cheerful to keep going. New York certainly has roots with Jewish comedians of Yiddish theatres of the Lower East Side, and New York continues to take in new forms as new residents arrive. This type of humour continues to inspire many New Yorkers, and theatres reflect its often-caustic comedic vein in new 'local' plays.

THE PEOPLE

New York City has flattened out in terms of population growth and, like London, now maintains a figure of above 7 million. These two cities, having long claimed to be the biggest in the world, are now far smaller than **São Paulo** in Brazil and **Mexico City**. Yet New York has always been diverse, always received the mass of new citizens, and it remains a mixture of many races. This is very evident from your first trip on the subway!

Over half of the population is white, about one-quarter is black, and there is a large sprinkling of Asians, as well as Native Americans. There's really no ethnic majority, but a number of minorities. **Hispanics** are now the most numerous in this grouping.

Of the original European settler groups, many still live in New York and, while not as numerous as they once were, the **Irish**, **Italian** and **Jewish** citizens do still make a vital and concerned contribution to city life and government. This is sometimes evident in specific areas: at one time half of the New York police force seemed to be Irish. More recent arrivals have been from the **Caribbean** (especially Puerto Rico and Haiti) and a considerable influx has also been received from **Russia**, **Central America**, **India** and **Southeast Asia**. New arrivals tend to group together. For example, you'll find many fruit and vegetable stands run by **Vietnamese** and **Koreans** on the Lower East Side.

Below: *Buskers in Manhattan do all sorts of tricks to attract the crowds.*

Language

Although to all intents English is the first language, Americans sometimes use different words to mean different things. You will find an example of these Americanisms on p. 123. Although you will have no difficulty in being understood in New York, **Spanish** has unmistakably made its mark and is a growing language. Signs on shops, boardings, subways and buses are catering more and more for Hispanics. The Spanish-speaking citizens, who are mostly from Puerto Rico, Cuba and South and Central America, have brought a new mixture and lively presence to this ever-changing city.

Apart from these two languages, there are many others to be heard as you walk around the principal streets. **Yiddish** was once prevalent, although less frequently heard now. **Greek**, **Italian**, **Russian** and **Turkish** have their own areas, and in Chinatown you can hear not one but several of the **Chinese** tongues.

Above: *A renewed police presence in New York helps to make the visitors feel more confident.*

Religion

Religions run the gamut of world beliefs, alongside all kinds of cults. Although long ago the established religion was essentially Protestant in its many forms, Catholicism is a big force, established by the immigrants from Ireland and Italy. New York's two most famous churches are **St John the Divine** and **St Patrick's**. There are many synagogues, mosques and temples. Whatever your belief, you will find some element of it in this city.

Festivals and Parades

There's hardly a week that goes by without some form of parade or celebration and these events tend to be big, gregarious and great fun. The **Columbus Day Parade** draws huge crowds. Whole areas may be transformed, whether they are for local festivals or big events. On **St Patrick's Day**, Fifth Avenue and even the flowers in their stands are coloured green, and the parade is received by dignitaries on the steps of St Patrick's Cathedral; and the locals of the East Village celebrate the **Ukrainian Festival** in May. The most famous is **San Gennaro's** in Little Italy,

NEW YORK'S FIRST ST PATRICK'S

St Patrick's Cathedral, an exercise in the Gothic Revival completed in 1888, stands in splendour on Fifth Avenue and provides an oasis for visitors from the hurry of the avenue outside. But it isn't the first St Patrick's in the city – to find that one you need to go to Little Italy on the Lower East Side and search out St Patrick's at 264 Mulberry Street. Here, damaged by fire in 1866, rather forlorn and needing a facelift, is the Gothic Revival original of 1815, seat of the first Catholic Archbishop of New York.

VISUAL ARTS

For painting and sculpture, stroll along East 57th Street, or nearby Madison Avenue, for the smartest and most expensive galleries, often specializing in particular artists and style. For new talents visit TriBeCa and its galleries or wander through West Chelsea. The **Frick Collection** and the **Metropolitan Museum of Art** have some of the most spectacular and famous works of art in the world.

OFF-BROADWAY

The dedicated theatre-goer in New York will always be sniffing around for the new and unusual. Broadway became arthritic long ago, and while it still turns out top musicals, straight and experimental drama has almost no place on the Great White Way. New and lively events in dance and mini-musicals, as well as drama, often take place in tiny, off-the-track spaces to be found all over the city. Some, like the **Manhattan Theater Club**, have become big, but there's a lot more out there. Ask around.

Right: *The Metropolitan Museum of Art. Spacious art galleries, both public and private, make NYC a leader in the art world.*

where you can nosh on Italian food as you parade under festive lights; and newly established Indian settlements (there are several 'Little Indias') offer Hindu celebrations such as **Diwali**. This is a major Hindu religious festival honouring the goddess of Wealth. It is characterized by feasting, presents and the lighting of lamps.

Many of these events are ethnic, yet wherever you come from, you will feel welcome. For dates and information on such events the Convention and Visitors' Bureau (*see* page 121) has listings.

The Arts

New York as a place just to eat, shop and indulge yourself wouldn't bring in many tourists, and with no arts the city would be a poor place. This is one of the liveliest and most creative places on the planet. Without **Broadway**, without magnificent museums, libraries and galleries, without book and record shops, without buzzing and intriguing centres of painting, sculpture and writing, without that incredible parade of architecture, there would indeed be very few reasons to come here. It's all going on non-stop in such vital centres as Midtown, Greenwich Village, SoHo, TriBeCa and the Upper West Side, with the added attraction of their parades of unusual characters.

Theatre

To find out what's on in Broadway, check newspapers and weekly arts guides. There are always the big musical and dramatic play hits, and these can be expensive, but there is a range of ticket prices and some bargains. The top talent performs on Broadway, from box office stars to supporting actors, dancers and singers,

directors and designers. Performances usually start on Tuesday and carry on to Sunday. Be sure to book.

The same goes for the lively movement known as Off-Broadway, which has a range of theatres all over Midtown and in the East and West Village. Often these smaller houses will have unusual, provocative plays with top artists and some, such as the lively **Manhattan Project**, often bring new shows to Broadway and beyond.

Literary New York

New York has always been a hive for writers, from the great names of the last century (**Henry James**, **Edith Wharton and Willa Cather**) to more recent literary luminaries like Don DeLillo. Many spent time away in Europe, but unfailingly drew on New York for experience and background. A number of hotels are famous for their associations: the **Algonquin** drew the wits of the 1920s and the **Chelsea Hotel** is currently a meeting place for playwrights and poets.

Many writers chose Greenwich Village as their preferred place and you will come across plaques on the various houses in which they lived. Today it's more likely that working writers will live on the Upper West Side, a place of old apartment buildings. It's a feisty area with a life of its own. There are also lots of bookshops and food emporiums along Upper Broadway.

Above: *Radio City Music Hall is a big attraction, and a monument to the Art Deco style.*

CHEAP SEATS

On **Times Square** is a very popular booth called **TKTS** where people queue every day for cheap tickets to shows. It offers a range of shows for off- and on-Broadway matinees and evening performances, day of the performance only, usually at half-price plus a small fee. Daily allocation of seats can be small, so some do sell out. Shows offered are indicated on notice boards, and can include some hits. Also sold at a new visitor centre in the old foyer of the Embassy Theatre, opposite TKTS on 7th Avenue, and another is at Front and John streets in South Street Seaport.

Music and Dance

New York is a music town and there is much of it here, from symphony concerts to recitals, band events and pop concerts. In summer, the parks have open-air concerts which are free and very popular. World-renowned **Carnegie Hall** is now the home of the NY Philharmonic, **Lincoln Center** offers packed programmes and don't neglect the **Juilliard School** for small events .

For major pop concerts, venues like **Madison Square Garden**, **Shea Stadium** and **Meadowlands**, or the prestigious **Avery Fisher Hall** cater for the crowds. For major black stars (and minor on Wednesday Amateur Night), the new-look **Apollo Theater** on West 125th Street is back in business. It features top entertainers performing the blues, gospel and jazz. Other live music venues include **The Beacon** on 74th St and **Irving Plaza**, 17 Irving Place. Check the freesheets or the *New York Times*, for current concert schedules.

The New York City Ballet is resident dance company at the State Theater. Like the Met, it is used by visiting companies when the principal occupant is touring or on leave. This company continues in the style of George Balanchine who founded it. An evening here can be very exciting.

As dance is such a big interest in New York there is much activity, from classical to modern and experimental. *See* alternative publications or the *Village Voice*.

Opera

The **Lincoln Center** is synonymous with opera and dance. One of the few companies to pursue an expensive repertory system is the **Metropolitan Opera**, with a different work on every night except Sundays. American Ballet Theatre is resident company and there are dance events when the opera season is not in progress.

Above: *Carnegie Hall hosts all kinds of concerts.*
Opposite top: *Bargains on- and off-Broadway at TKTS Booth on Times Square. Day of performance sales only.*

The style of the Greek Revival, last seen in the early 19th century, returned in the first decade of the 20th century. Alas, Pennsylvania Station, a grandiose Greek temple, has gone, replaced by **Madison Square Garden**, but you can still feel those expansive times in the marble halls of **Grand Central Terminal** on East 42nd Street. Later came many upshooting buildings (both the **Empire State** and the **Chrysler** buildings, elegant epitomes of the **Art Deco** style, date from this time). New building and the desire to impress resulted in architectural booms with New York being a mirror of many styles.

Architecture

It is hard to find much in New York that pre-dates the mid-19th century. In the East Village and Chelsea, in Lower Manhattan, you'll discover a few early and often isolated examples of **Federal** architecture from redbrick residences to the first brownstones. You will also find some later, interesting architectural styles, notably the cast-iron fronted warehouse buildings of SoHo. There was a flowering of exotic factory and office buildings 150 years ago and there are examples along lower Broadway and a few in the Financial District. In addition, there are some splendid examples of the **Art Deco** period that flourished during the opulent 1920s. These exotically sculpted, sometimes gilded and tiled buildings can be found all over the city, but particularly in Midtown. If you only take in one example of the style, look for them at **Rockefeller Center** and **Radio City Music Hall**, or eat at the **Waldorf-Astoria** or the stunning restaurant at the **Essex House Hotel**.

New York shines in modern buildings too, mostly imperious glass-and-steel shafts noted for their pure simplicity. A recent exotic addition is the **Four Seasons Hotel**, which rises like a stern Egyptian temple on 57th Street, its corners knobbed with light fixtures like perched vultures. Try the two new Ritz Carlton hotels (one at Ground Zero), elegant and containing utter luxury within.

Below: *Art Deco is every-where. Look for small elegant details too, both inside and out.*

Above: *Baseball is America's summer sport and popular with kids.*
Opposite: *Food on roadside stands looks and smells good. But choose carefully.*

Sport and Recreation

New York is a major centre for all sports, though the popular ones such as baseball (April–October) and American Football (August–December) are outstanding. **The Mets** (the local baseball team) move to Citi Field, Willets Point, in 2009, the New York Yankees to the new Yankee Stadium in the Bronx, also in 2009. Football is played at the Giants' Stadium in Rutherford, New Jersey, and the teams are the **Giants** and the **Jets**. Note that tickets for these events are very hard to come by.

Basketball, also very popular (November–April), has one main team, the **Knickerbockers**, or 'Knicks', at Madison Square Garden. Ice Hockey teams (October–April) are the **New York Rangers** and the **New Jersey Devils**, the former at Madison Square Garden.

Other sports are available to the visitor in bewildering array. You can go bowling or boating, running or rollerblading, swimming or skating. You can play golf, squash or tennis, and there are fitness classes on offer all over town. There's horse riding in Central Park and in Brooklyn, as well as several race tracks. Riding and exercise trails in Brooklyn and the suburbs can be found in the city's parks and beaches.

HORSE RACING

New Yorkers love 'a flutter' (they love to bet), and their tastes are well catered for, with several tracks close to the city reachable on public transport. You can catch where there's horse racing on local radio stations. Popular are Aqueduct with a season from October–May, and Belmont Park with thoroughbred flat racing May–July and September–October. The track at Meadowlands in East Rutherford, New Jersey, also has that unusual sport of trotting from January–August and is open Monday–Saturday.

Food and Drink

New York is one of those great gastronomic centres where the food range is enormous. It has some of the best food in the world and there are many very good restaurants, mainly in Midtown, Chinatown and the Village. New York is a city of many styles and a place where **French food** really *is* French and not an imitation, as so often happens. Many French restaurateurs have moved to the city, particularly **Bretons**, and have opened upper-crust establishments, often luring leading French chefs to join their team.

There are also small and comfortable eateries where you can obtain a set-price meal that might make you feel you were in a lively French provincial city, if it weren't for the roar of the New York traffic just beyond the door.

Other than French and hearty native New York food (and there's nothing better, from the fresh seafood of Long Island to luscious Caesar salads, or steaks from the Midwest), there's a mouth-watering selection of different foods that you could sample for months and still not have gone through the whole menu. Add to these many small neighbourhood diners where a good breakfast can be very cheap – and a waitress will refill your cup at no extra charge. Children will love these straightforward American places which are popular with the locals and Americans visiting out-of-town. You can either sit at the counter or at tables and eat well-filled sandwiches or truly fat and mouth-watering hamburgers.

If you are on a budget, eating can be very cheap if you live on hot dogs or salads. Food and drink, particularly for light eating, has improved in the stations. Try the famous (but expensive) **Oyster Bar** at Grand Central. There are many food stalls and barrows in street corners, offering cheap snacks. For coffee and conversation, the new places are the bookshops, where you'll find refreshment areas among the shelves, and these new arrivals stay open till late.

There's good news if you plan to eat around the Broadway theatre and cabaret area. The Theater District in the **west 40s** is undergoing a revival. **Eighth Avenue** is being cleaned up with a section devoted to restaurants. Newly revamped hotels in the area are smartening up too: the **Paramount** and the **Millennium** offer a chance to eat right in the midst of things.

American rail stations can be exotic: Art Deco palaces such as Los Angeles and Cincinnatti Ohio, and truly grandiose **Grand Central** on East 42nd Street. Grand Central does not serve cross-country routes (as does Pennsylvania Station, now a series of underground vaults), but nevertheless it is a New York marvel. It now has a smart market for fish, meat and vegetables – good for self-caterers. Eat and drink here at the unique, or at chain places, like Starbucks. Try Michael Jordan's Steakhouse, or snack at Junior's Cheesecake, Cipriani Dolci, or enjoy cocktails at The Campbell Apartment.

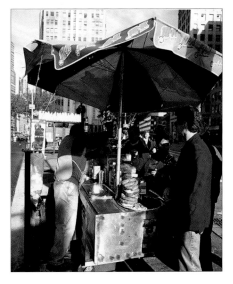

Opposite: *NY bars are popular with locals and, besides drinks, bar food is usually good.*

Below: *There's one word for Chinatown: crowded. Even the restaurants have moved off the street and on to upper floors.*

If there's one place you shouldn't miss it's **Chinatown**, where there are a vast number of Oriental styles and dishes. This once tight area, north of the Financial district, has expanded and is now very large. There is every type of restaurant available, from the cheap to the flamboyant, all mixed in with shops, markets and bars. It is hard to go wrong here, and prices are usually not that expensive. If it's a snack, dinner, or day-long dim sum you are after, you'll find it here. The city's Chinatown is a paradise for eaters, and highly recommended by local food critics too. Be warned: this is New York and writing about food and drink can be as arcane and folly ridden as some London or Paris reviews. Restaurants come and go quickly.

Next-door to Chinatown in **Little Italy** you can eat well, but bear in mind the food here is **Southern Italian**. Most immigrants came from Sicily and the south so it's solid pasta-and-heavy-tomato-sauce fare, and it's not cheap either. Look for seasonal celebrations in the city when food stalls are set up and you can try local snacks from Greek to Ukrainian or Cuban to Haitian, depending on the district. In New York the soul food (such as ribs, greens, corn bread, muffins and black-eyed beans) of the black community is worth trying too.

ETHNIC RESTAURANTS

It's not so long ago that it wasn't easy to find a good Indian restaurant in the city, but the influx of Asians has changed all that. They have been matched by Cubans, Koreans, Vietnamese, Thais, Japanese, Haitians, Central Americans and Russians, all bringing their own cuisines and an accompanying nostalgia for the food of their country. You may need to seek your selection out (Russia, for example, is centred by the sea in an area known as Little Odessa), but the choice of foods is amazing.

Drinks and Bars

Drinking in New York is a dream, whether your tipple is wine, beer, or those wondrous cocktails mixed with verve that really taste of liquor and give an instant heady glow. You can have straight drinks in your hotel bar, romantic cocktails in lofty settings overlooking Manhattan, or dip into neighbourhood bars where half the clientele will be watching a game on the ubiquitous TV. Irish bars abound, especially along Second and Third Avenues, and probably the most atmospheric one is McSorley's in the Village, a classic hangout, but many others offer good beer, local and imported, as well as live music and jazz.

Another good thing about New York is that whatever atmosphere you are looking for in a bar, you will find. Bars vary: from singles to sophisticated, arty to odd, theatrical caves or thumping musical dives, gregarious to gay. The selection is enormous and it is changing all the time. The opening hours can go on forever: often, closing-time merely means the doors shut in the early morning hours from 04:00–06:00 in order to clean up the joint. As a result many bars don't get going until very late at night, especially at weekends. If this is your scene, you could be in heaven.

TABLE TALK

- **à la mode:** with ice cream.
- **bagel:** chewy bread roll often served with lox (smoked salmon) and cream cheese.
- **broiled:** grilled.
- **dim sum:** a parade of tiny steamed dumplings filled with meat, fish or vegetables.
- **eggs:** ask for them 'sunny side up' and they'll be fried on one side only; 'over easy', fried quickly on both sides.
- **egg cream:** delicious concoction of iced milk, chocolate syrup and soda water.
- **hash browns:** fried potatoes with onion.
- **hero:** French bread sandwich.
- **jerk:** hot barbecued pork or chicken.
- **knish:** savoury dough filled with cheese or potato.
- **pretzel:** savoury bread twist sold on street corners.
- **check:** bill.

2
Lower Manhattan

The tip of Manhattan Island is where New York City was born three centuries ago, but there's very little of that early past left. Of the first Dutch settlements nothing remains, and of the British Colonial era very little. As New York prospered in the 18th century many handsome residential buildings were built here; few survive, though the restored **Fraunces Tavern** on Pearl Street will give some idea of what the early city looked like.

Much of Lower Manhattan is infill from the time the Dutch started to break down hills, flatten out building areas, or to dig canals. They started a process which has never stopped, the most intriguing development will be what replaces the vanished World Trade Center. During the turbulent times of building, rebuilding, filling in land and building yet again, to arrive at the towers of the modern city of today, much has been swept away in the name of progress. In the eager haste to make money history has always slipped to a back place, and only comparatively recently has the city taken any pride in its exciting and fast-moving past.

What you see now is a business city, rather like the city of London but with fewer residents, receiving a huge influx of office workers every day. The **Financial District** stands firmly on old New York: with only tiny islands of the old, like St Paul's Chapel. As the Financial District ends, the sleek corporate skyscrapers are replaced by old warehouses and piers, now restored as the **South Street Seaport**. The Civic Center, a hive of government buildings and law courts, lies nearby.

DON'T MISS

*** Statue of Liberty: New York's symbol of freedom.
*** Ground Zero: since 2001 the Twin Towers site has become a pilgrimage.
*** Staten Island Ferry: for the best views in NY.
** South Street Seaport: a lively, living museum.
** Battery Park: has a superb waterfront view.
* Ellis Island: retells the story of American immigrants.

Opposite: *A glorious gift to the USA from France in the 1880s, the Statue of Liberty is spectacular.*

THE BEST OF LOWER MANHATTAN

Without doubt, after Midtown, this is one of the most popular parts of Manhattan for visitors. Apart from exploring, it is also a magnificent sight, whether seen from a ferry, from Brooklyn Heights, or from a helicopter.

Battery Park ★★

At the foot of Manhattan Island is Battery Park, a green space of 21 acres (8.5ha) that's also a result of infill. There are marvellous harbour views. The park takes its name from the line-up of cannons once surmounting the nearby circular stone fort. Boats leave for the Statue of Liberty, Ellis Island and Staten Island from the park's docks.

Castle Clinton National Monument ★

Like its twin, **Castle William**, on Governor's Island at the East Battery, Castle Clinton was built in 1808 to protect the city. When peace and independence made the fortress redundant, it was roofed over and became a music hall. Among the stars of the day who performed, the 'Swedish nightingale', Jenny Lind, sang for the first time in America here in 1850. In 1896 Castle Clinton became the **New York Aquarium** (now in Brooklyn) but today is a National Historic Monument with exhibits on the history of New York. Open 08:30–17:00 daily, www.nps.gov/cacl

Statue of Liberty ★★★

A gift from the French, Liberty, a magnificent work by French sculptor Frédéric Bartholdi, and now the symbol of New York, almost didn't make it. She nearly foundered at sea, and on arrival had to wait in huge chunks to be assembled, then for money to be raised by donations

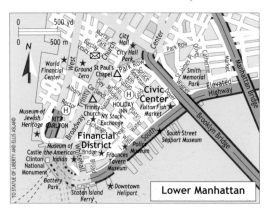

Lower Manhattan

before being raised on her pedestal in 1886. The statue is 305ft (93m) high from ground to torch. Pedestal, museum and grounds open to tours. Free tickets. (Ferry tickets from Battery Park charged.) After a long restoration, it's still uncertain whether one will be able to go inside this National Monument. www.nps.gov/stli

Ellis Island *

This is a national monument to the more than 17 million New Americans who arrived here between 1892 and 1954. A major

refurbishment has provided this one-time entry point with attractions dealing with the island's adaptation and also a complete history of the new arrivals. It touchingly retells the story of the great immigration which began in the mid-19th century. The History Center (www.ellisisland.org) has all the records and a Wall of Honor of over 400 000 notable immigrants. Live acts and a gift shop in summer. Open 08:30–16:00 daily.

Above: *These stern halls on an isolated island once confronted all immigrants. Now they house a fascinating museum on this vital aspect of US history.*

Staten Island Ferry ***

A great harbour experience, the Ferry is free for Whitehall Terminal for foot passengers. You get a marvellous sight-seeing voyage of the **Statue of Liberty** and **Ellis Island**, and when crossing the harbour, you see the maritime traffic crowding the water. Disembark from the ferry and explore the large and tranquil Staten Island (see p. 105) and look back to the grand spectacle of Manhattan rising from the waves. www.nyc.gov/dot

Below: *The old Staten Island ferries, serving commuters, make a great free ride.*

Museum of the American Indian *

Behind the ornate façade of the **United States Custom House** on Bowling Green lies this interesting museum, with one of the largest collections of material concerning Native Americans in the world. It forms part of the **Smithsonian Institution** and is a fascinating repository of artefacts from most of the hundreds of tribes that once inhabited the huge area we know now as the United States. Open 10:00–17:00 daily.

Ground Zero ***

By 2012 a new World Trade Center will dominate the Manhattan skyline. The centrepiece will be the 1766ft (538m) high Freedom Tower with four other high risers and a memorial centre nearby. Skirt the gravestones of the defiant **St Paul's chapel**, which honours the victims of 9/11, to view developments; alternatively, survey the scene from the dazzling glass atrium of the **Winter Garden** in the Financial Center building. Other developments include Battery Park.

OTHER MUSEUMS AND PLACES OF INTEREST

There are several other fascinating museums in this part of Manhattan. Look out for the **Museum of Jewish Heritage**, a Star of David-shaped building just north of Battery Park housing material concerning the Holocaust. In the Federal Hall National Memorial is the **Museum of American Constitutional Government**. In Old Slip there's a **Police Museum**. The **Whitney Museum** has decamped back to its main quarters on 42nd Street. Outdated government buildings, banks and offices are being recycled as well.

FRAUNCES TAVERN

This handsome brick Georgian building, with its colonial air, is actually a fake. This is because it is a replica of the original tavern which was built in 1719. However, it still retains a sense of what it must have been like in 1783, when General Washington made a farewell speech to his officers here. There are spacious rooms with fireplaces; you can also eat and drink in 'Colonial style' here during the working week. Upstairs is a museum on the War of Independence. Open 12:00–17:00 Mon–Sat.

Among the banks and businesses, note **One Wall Street** which has an impressive Art Deco banking hall, and the **Federal Reserve Bank**. Like the City of London, churches are really the only old buildings remaining. **Trinity Church**, right in the middle on Broadway at Wall Street, with its graveyard is one example (over 150 years old, it is the third church on the site). **St Paul's Chapel** is the oldest (built not long after its London model, St Martin-in-the-Fields, in 1766) and contains Washington's own private pew.

See also the **US Courthouse** with its gold pyramidal roof on Foley Square and the **New York Stock Exchange** at Broad Street. Visitors used to be able to watch the busy stock and bond traders from a gallery which overlooks the trading floor, but the Exchange is no longer open to visitors. Also noteworthy is the **Federal Hall National Monument**, a version of the Parthenon in the finest Greek Revival style. Although it wasn't built when he took the oath, a statue of **George Washington** before it marks the spot where he became president in 1789.

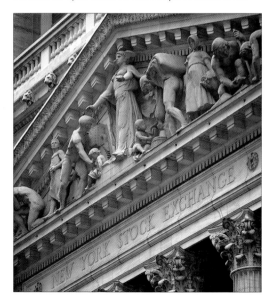

Opposite: *The Financial Center's Winter Garden is a very popular place to eat.* **Left:** *In Lower Manhattan modern glass and steel contrast with reproductions of classic styles.*

CORRUPTION IN THE CITY

In City Hall Park is a handsome 19th-century stone building, **Tweed Courthouse**. When it was built in 1862 a great part of the cash it cost was funnelled straight into 'Boss' Tweed's corrupt political machine. Heading Tammany Hall, his autocratic rule in the 1860s was synonymous with extreme greed. The plundering of public funds ran into millions. Eventually there was so much anger at the blatant profiteering of Tweed's party that it was terminated in 1871 by the exposures in the *New York Times*. The Courthouse is now the HQ for NYC Schools Administration.

THE CIVIC CENTER AND SOUTH STREET SEAPORT

The **Civic Center** is an enclave of government buildings, a curiously mixed set, towards the north of the area. It is bordered by the **Financial District** and **Chinatown** (*see* pp. 44–45). Set in a green and paved open space, the curiously small **City Hall** is to be found here. Its staff and offices overspill into the nearby **Municipal Building**, with its fanciful roof decorations. This is a business area, but now, with gardens, fountains and Ground Zero visitors, is also busy at weekends.

City Hall *

The City Hall is a grand building, its style described as Baroque and Renaissance with Federal touches. There are lots of fanciful flourishes on this building! Completed in 1811, it is still the centre of New York City's government. Unfortunately, one is no longer allowed inside to see its many treasures. City Hall used to be sheathed with marble on three sides, but not on the north side: at the time of its construction nobody could foresee how the city would spread beyond it. After the 1956 restoration, it was completely refaced in limestone. The surrounding space is **City Hall Park**, once the village green of the growing city.

South Street Seaport **

At Fulton and South Streets, an evocative sight not to be missed is the South Street Seaport. Allow a lot of time to see this large place which has many aspects. A long-term project to mark the city's vital maritime history (it was founded because of the fine harbour), this 11-square block project well commemorates a time when New York was sovereign of the sea. Goods arrived from around the world and from the birth of the new country, trade increased with a fierce vitality. New York is still the East Coast's premier port.

In its great days South Street was a forest of masts and tackle, an image this very good 'living' museum attempts to perpetuate. Aside from visiting the seven sailing ships moored here, all meticulously restored, you can actually sail on one, the *Pioneer*, a schooner dating from 1885, or take harbour cruises on the replicas of old craft often in the evening for music and drinks. **Circle Line** and **Seaport Liberty** ships go from Pier 16 and offer a 60-minute narrated trip. Free events from jazz to street acts. www.southstreetseaportmuseum.org

The Old Docks **

Around South Street was a seething waterside dock area which has totally vanished. You can recapture some of the feeling of those lively, dangerous days in the nearby restored 19th-century buildings containing maritime exhibitions, an archaeological presentation at 17 State Street called **New York Unearthed**, and a 19th-century print shop and a children's centre. In the early 19th-century **Schermerhorn Row** are modern shops on the ground floor, as well as ships' chandlers and examples of sea-life providers. Surrounding streets are intriguing too.

This old chunk of Manhattan is renovated to appear as it once was. Well recommended for a real New York ramble with over 100 new shops and eateries along Fulton to Pier 17, yet it still gives a sense of the old dockside. See also the **Battery Maritime Building** on South Street, a surviving example of a ferry dock from before the opening of the **Brooklyn Bridge** when scores of boats carried people back and forth across to Brooklyn. There is also the **Fulton Fish Market** which still sells fish, with guided tours if you want to see it in operation (check for opening times).

Above: *An apt impression of Brooklyn Bridge over the East River. You can walk across for grand views.*
Opposite: *South Street Seaport isn't just a museum, there are lots of shops too.*

BROOKLYN BRIDGE

A handsome arch over the East River, and a New York legend, the Brooklyn Bridge was a 19th-century marvel. It went through many changes and there were many fatalities, including its creator, John Augustus Roebling. It opened in 1883 and took 14 years to build. The total span is almost 1600ft (488m) and it's a major artery feeding into Lower Manhattan, carrying many New York commuters every day. It's also a grandstand for pedestrians to view the river craft and the skyline from elevated footways.

3
Lower East Side and East Village

This is where the first immigrants were shifted as their numbers grew. Landlords saw the possibility of cheap housing sites on the marshes east of the Bowery (then an undeveloped and unhealthy area), which together with the East Village south of 14th Street, makes up the Lower East Side belt. Hundreds of thousands of new settlers were herded into the low-lying area bounded by Lower Manhattan around **Canal Street** with **East Houston Street** to the north and the Bowery to the west. The two areas now have quite separate personalities.

This unwelcoming site was their introduction to a new life, but most immigrants didn't despair. They worked hard, made enough money to get out and moved on. Like the huge transit camp it has always been, the area still has a mean and despairing air. Take care when visiting as some sections away from the major avenues are not very safe. The young, however, flock here and it is increasingly becoming the hip place to be.

The **Chinese** are still here, and so are the **Italians**, with well-marked areas of their own. The **Irish** were the first to put down roots, followed by **German**, **Jewish**, **Polish** and **Greek** influxes. The area has always been a migratory area and most recently it has been the **Hispanics** who have moved in, and with them people from the **Caribbean** islands. Many moved on, but it is still home for many **Puerto Ricans**, **African-Americans** and the Chinese. Indeed Chinatown has developed so rapidly it has taken over large parts of Little Italy and the Jewish Lower East Side.

DON'T MISS

*** Chinatown: it's big, run-down and decrepit in parts, but has marvellous food.
* Cooper Union: school and gallery in a handsome brownstone building.
* Little Italy: still here, though smaller; you can get solid Italian food here.
* Lafayette Street: here you'll find the Colonnade and the Public Theater.
* Orchard Street: a renowned market; everything is cheap.

Opposite: *Chinatown is filled with restaurants and gaudy neon signs.*

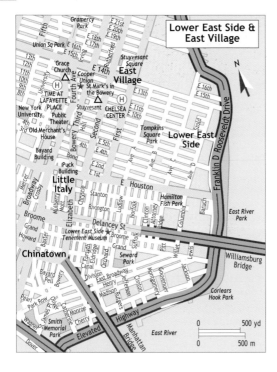

Lower East Side & East Village

LOWER EAST SIDE

A site for many festivals, from **Chinese New Year** to **San Gennaro**, the Lower East Side can for a time shed its unattractive image of packed old buildings and dilapidated shops and put on a show. But it is still an area of deprivation and poverty, so go by day and be prepared for a walk on the sad side.

The area is still the first stop for new immigrants, and it used to be a predominantly Jewish area. They were crammed into the newly erected apartment buildings, and the area had plenty of synagogues. At one time it was the largest Jewish settlement in the world as arrivals flooded in from the pogroms of Russia, dispossession in Hungary and Romania and, most recently, after persecution in Nazi Germany in the 1930s. The Lower East Side is now home to closely integrated settlements of Asians, Hispanics and Jews.

Cashing in on the need for homes, from the middle of the 19th century developers rapidly constructed buildings that still line the streets today. Glad to find any roof, the new arrivals were crammed in. Many buildings had no running water and families had to share small apartments. In this lively, overcrowded area money was scarce, so it's not surprising that, aside from being a cheap place to live, bargain shopping has developed. On **Canal Street**, **Houston** and surroundings, there are many cheap shops and stalls, often overflowing on to the sidewalks.

A, B, C, D ...

Alphabet City on the eastern edge of this area is even more desolate in parts. This section, where avenues are lettered, was a drug centre and remains largely run down, with battered and sometimes ruined blocks spreading between Avenues A to D. Residents here try hard to rehabilitate and inject a feeling of community. There's a sculpture garden, and lively poetry readings are held at the Nuyorican Poets Café.

Left: Street markets selling all kinds of goods can be found everywhere. Orchard Street is very popular.
Below: Most New Yorkers live on top of each other, in apartments. Alphabet City is particularly crowded and insalubrious.

Orchard Street *

The place most people head for is Orchard Street, between Delancy Street and East Houston Street. If you don't mind the crowds and the harried salespeople, then you'll enjoy it. Orchard Street is the ultimate New York place for discount shopping for just about everything, but particularly clothes and fabrics, household goods and hardware. It's very busy on Sundays, as it was originally a market set up by Jewish merchants. Some shops are still shuttered on Saturdays, but new arrivals, including young designers and entrepreneurs of all races, are reviving it.

Lower East Side Tenement Museum *

First built in 1856 on Orchard Street as the immigrant wave grew, this apartment building was one of many first homes for New Americans and is now listed as a National Historic Landmark. Within, you will find apartments of the era, some left exactly as they were when landlords turned the key on departing residents a century ago. The museum is accessible by guided tours only: 13:00–16:45 Tuesday–Friday, 11:00–16:45 Saturday–Sunday.

The Bowery

People used to drive fast along the wide thoroughfare that is the Bowery, when old boozers would try to clean your windows with filthy rags. It is fast changing, less of a resort for the derelicts and dropouts of New York, though some still spend their time panhandling the streets, sleeping rough, and in the stark cold of winter huddled figures cluster over pavement gratings emitting a little warmth.

Although its name has a romantic origin (from the Dutch *bouwerie*, or a country lane, which it was until New York's surge north) this main street up to the East Village, along with First and Second avenues, can be grim. Yet it remains a place some tourists want to see. Its appeal must lie solely in seeing the dregs of an opulent city. True, the spread of theatre activity in New York has brought small playhouses and cafés to unlikely places, and you will find a smattering of theatre, dance and performance art here. There are also cut-price stores and renovated loft apartments. In general, however, the Bowery is still an indictment of our uncaring society.

There are some interesting buildings in the neighbourhood and both main avenues and side streets reveal impressive commercial buildings, some of them cast-iron and others with decorative brickwork. Look for the **Bayard Building** (Bleecker at Crosby Street) and, a bit further south, the home of a one-time humour magazine, the **Puck Building**. This has droll sculptures of the famous imp, top-hatted and mirror in hand, on the corner and over the door of numbers 295–309 Lafayette Street.

Little Italy *

Once Canal Street was the border between Chinatown and Little Italy, but this area is shrinking as the old folk fade away and younger Italo-Americans are more likely to be up at Arthur Avenue in the Bronx. Chinatown, the southern neighbour, is cutting across Canal Street as it expands and encroaches.

Little Italy still has an air of Southern Italy (Naples and Sicily, predominantly, as most immigrants came from there) and lots of places to eat filling meals. **Mulberry Street** is its main street, where the stress is more on heavy Sicilian styles and quantity (often vast dishes of pasta and a thick tomato dressing known as 'red sauce') than quality. Try **Luna** at no. 112 which is cheap and popular enough to cause queues, and **Angelo's** at no. 146 for solid southern dishes. Cafés offer Italian coffee and pastries.

Above: *Restaurants provide big pasta meals (often Sicilian) in Little Italy.*

Little Italy is a very good area to go shopping. The food stores have plenty of salamis, freshly made pastas, cheeses and other imported delicacies. The most exciting time to visit is during the **Festival of San Gennaro** on 19 September when floats fill the streets, stands offer filling foods and the place is all lit up.

Below: *Unlike its neighbours, Chinatown grows and burgeons.*

Chinatown ★★★

This is one of the most fascinating areas of New York. Chinatown, at the southern edge of the Lower East Side, is many things to many people and one thing is sure: you can eat very well indeed here. But this is New York, so forget the large and well-ordered Chinese communities in London, Vancouver or San Francisco. This one is, by comparison, a mess.

It's fearfully crowded, grimy with cracked neon lights and disintegrating brick façades. But what a place – it's both smelly and sophisticated, and it is real. As

Above: Chinatown is
a lively mix of eateries,
shops and even places
of worship, like this
Mott Street temple.

PLACES TO EAT

Ducks hang everywhere
in Chinese restaurants
and the food smells in
Chinatown are intoxicating.
There are lots of places to
choose from, especially
around Mott Street and
Grand Street, up to the
Bowery, but your best bet is
to look for ones that the
Chinese eat in. If you like
wine with your meal you
may need to bring your
own. Also along Broadway,
you will find low-priced
snack bars of all kinds,
featuring both American and
Jewish as well as new
menus from incoming Asian
and Caribbean arrivals.

many as 150,000 Chinese
live and work between
the confines of the
Bowery and Broadway,
and many more of their
relations from all over the
Metropolitan Area come
'back home' on week-
ends. It was originally a
defined area, now over-
spilling on all sides.

The heart of the com-
munity is **Mott Street,** a
restaurant alley with all sorts of eateries. Although the
area is mainly Cantonese, you can find excellent
Shanghai-, Pekingese- and Szechwan-style food. You
can also eat from stalls and fill up on intriguing snacks.
Eating can be a real bargain here, with plenty of choice
and lots of special menus displayed to lure you in.

It's a pity not to indulge in Chinese foods and if you're
not sure what to order, there are many dim sum restaurants. These give you a chance to sample tiny servings,
often hot, often spicy, of a beguiling range of sometimes
mysterious specialities. You are charged by the dish, usually piled up in little baskets. Dim sum houses serve from
morning to mid-afternoon. Other places go from cheap
to charming, decorated with florid, gilded dragons, fans,
flowers, lanterns and figurines. Go at night when their
multi-coloured neon signs compete with each other.

Shops selling all the usual Oriental merchandise,
from scrolls and silk shoes and saucepans to kites and
cricket cages and chopsticks, are sandwiched in
these narrow streets. Upstairs rooms are often club-
rooms. There's a temple with gilt buddhas on **Mott
Street**, as well as the Chinatown Fair which is an
amusement arcade. The fair used to have a famous
curiosity: its dancing and game-playing live chickens.
Chinatown is a place with a life all of its own, and
even the telephone booths are capped with painted
and gilded pagodas.

EAST VILLAGE

Though well-known to New Yorkers, for visitors this is an amorphous area. The East Village is basically an extension of the Lower East Side, lying to the north, east from Fourth Avenue. Broadway and the Bowery are the two main north–south avenues.

More seedy, more raffish and much less charming or affluent than Greenwich Village itself, the East Village has served as a place where the less famous artist can live and still be near his or her preferred locality, although some have already been priced out. There are good reasons for a visit, though New Yorkers may try to put you off. It's safe enough in this part, but even so it's unwise to stray into too empty cross streets, especially after dark. This is basically a poor working quarter. Take care and stay on the well-lit main avenues. It's a place for new music, bizarre fashions and unusual gear. On some of the avenues are outrageous clothes and unusual antique and record shops which are often open late into the night.

The area abounds in historical connections. **St Mark's in the Bowery** on East 10th Street stands on the site of the chapel used by Peter Stuyvesant. **Cooper Union** is the birthplace of the NAACP (National Association for the Advancement of Coloured Peoples) and the American Red Cross. On Second Avenue above Houston are **Stars of**

MUSEUM OF CHINESE IN THE AMERICAS

If you want to know more about the Chinese – see the displays of Sino-American history; photographs of Chinese life in the USA, or take a walking tour of the area – then go to the **Museum of Chinese in the Americas** on Mulberry and Bayard. This is an interesting centre for serious study of the phenomenon of Chinatown. There is a library that can be used and a bookshop. Open 12:00–18:00 Tue–Sun.

WINING AND DINING

There's lots of choice for eating and drinking in the East Village, and many unusual places to choose from. It's noted for old-style bars such as **McSorley's Old Ale House** on East 7th Street, which claims to be the oldest in the country. Ethnic food abounds. There's still an **Italian** presence, with pastry shops north of 10th Street, and **Polish** restaurants. The strong **Ukrainian** flavour is reinforced by the restaurants as well as the annual festival which is held in May along East 7th Street, around the Ukrainian Church of St George. On East Sixth Street is another enclave of Indian settlers with many enticing restaurants.

Left: *Street life is a vital aspect of the East Village – you'll notice lots of graffiti spraypainted on the walls.*

THE COLONNADE

Originally a terrace of 13 stately town residences on Lafayette Place, this Greek Revival (1820s) row with its soaring pillars shows how grand the area once was. It has been cut in half and now only a section remains. Though sadly shabby and neglected, the area is looking up and the Colonnade still retains a patrician air.

Opposite top: *Originally Jewish, the bagel can be a snack meal.*
Opposite bottom: *Look out for the Greek Revival and cast-iron façades. This one is on Lafayette Street.*
Below: *New York's free libraries contain great literary treasures beside books!*

David in the pavement with the names of Jewish stage performers who once were seen in the vanished Yiddish-speaking theatres here. Later literary stars such as Jack Kerouac and Allen Ginsberg were residents, establishing the Beat Generation. Note the unusual motifs and the stone sculptures fashioned in ancient styles over the doors and windows of many otherwise very ordinary buildings.

Lafayette Place *

As an indication of city changes, Astor Place is intriguing. Local streets are becoming the new 'in' places to be. At Lafayette Place you'll find **The Colonnade**, where many famous people, including the novelists Washington Irving and Charles Dickens, lodged. Also on the wide street, the handsome old Astor Library is now the **Public Theater**, home of the New York Shakespeare Festival. Here many new and unusual productions have been seen, some transferring to Broadway. *Hair* and *A Chorus Line* started here. A great New Yorker, the late Joseph Papp struggled to maintain this institution (he was also responsible for initiating free performances of Shakespeare plays in Central Park). Enter its impressive lobbies and find out what is playing.

Old Merchant's House *

This unusual Federal-style residence was saved from destruction at 29 East 4th Street. It's a solitary example of how many streets once were, and how affluent families lived during the 19th century. The house is over 160 years old and has been carefully renovated as a typical family home of the period. Open 12:00–17:00 Thursday–Monday, closed Tuesday–Wednesday.

Cooper Union *

A striking brownstone building on **Cooper Square**, this classic New York institution was set up by philanthropist Peter Cooper, a self-educated man who started this free technical and arts college in 1859. It was also the first college for adult education and the first in the US to be racially integrated. There is a gallery for exhibitions of American history and design. Open 11:00–19:00 Monday–Friday, 12:00–17:00 Saturday.

Grace Church *

This lovely church was founded at a time when the area was still a smart place to live. It is hard to credit now, but there are still elegant brick houses on the cross streets around this imposing church on Broadway and 10th Street. Built mainly to serve wealthy Episcopal parishioners, the ornate steeple, recently restored, is a local landmark. A later marble addition replaced a wooden one even though it was thought that it would be too heavy for the church. Begun in 1843 and built in Gothic Revival style, this church gained for its designer, James Renwick, the contract to build the new St Patrick's Roman Catholic cathedral. He was only 23 when he designed Grace Church, yet it is considered to be his finest achievement. Opening hours vary. Always crowded, **St Mark's Place** (the name for 8th Street beyond Third Avenue) has dives playing new music, shops with a mix of low chic and second-hand clothes and punk gear. The place is alive far into the night. Here are trendy clubs and small restaurants of all sorts, mainly grungy and rundown. Along with punk and rock, folk and jazz all pulse loudly from the Bowery to the broad arrow of First Avenue.

North of 6th Street is the famous **Tompkins Square Park** where riots occurred in 1991 when homeless people were evicted because they had taken over the area. It has since been cleaned up and renovated, and is now a popular gathering place. Though it's not wise to hang about, there are good small shops around it. Read the anti-drug graffiti and look at the murals. Also check for newly placed historic site plaques.

> ### New Life For Old
>
> The 19th century was a time for the development of factories in Lower Manhattan. Many used cheap cast-iron construction, and façades were adorned with classical pillars and ornamental details. Originally built for commerce, the buildings are now in demand for expensive hotels, residences and loft apartments.

4
Greenwich Village, SoHo and TriBeCa

Get ready for some unusual experiences, visions and fantasies! No, it's not New York's version of tinseltown Hollywood, this is life among real artists. Although more realistic and perhaps not as pretty as the Puccini opera, versions of *La Bohème* are going on all over this city, but especially in some favoured areas. **Greenwich Village**, **SoHo** and **TriBeCa** are three neighbouring areas where artists, from painters and sculptors, to film-makers and performers, live and work. Every day the tourist tide floods through, having heard that this is the place for unusual sights that you certainly won't see anywhere else in the United States. In this part of town you won't be on your own with just a guide book for company – certainly not on a weekend. Art is big in New York and the city is a vital part of the international art city circuit. These areas are where the work is actually done.

The art movement started in **Greenwich Village.** It began as a real village (hence its name) before the flow of development engulfed it. But when the village became too expensive, artists moved to **SoHo** (South of Houston) in the early 1970s. As always happens, artists were soon followed by the crowd that wants to live like them without the pain of being poor, so the next area of decrepit commercial buildings to be taken over was TriBeCa, West Chelsea, or Triangle Below Canal Street. Even this rundown place is becoming fashionable. TriBeCa not only has fabulous galleries but also has very good, trendy restaurants on offer. However, the fortunate artists who got there first are still very much around.

Opposite: *For many New Yorkers recently renovated Washington Square Arch is the symbol of the Village.*

CABARET TIME!

The Village saw the blossoming of some of the first small theatres away from Broadway. Off-Broadway is well represented. So is Off-Off-Broadway, with cheaper spaces in less wholesome parts. Some of these theatres present quite surprising shows, although it's difficult to shock the neighbours. But this is the place for lively cafés and cabaret entertainment, and you can find plenty of small stages with stand-up comics, musicians and singers trying out their act.

GREENWICH VILLAGE

'The Village', as it is known, goes from **Houston Street** in the south to **14th Street** in the north, and from the **Hudson River** to **Fifth Avenue**, although its atmosphere continues beyond Fourth Avenue into what locals call 'the East Village', which is less respectable, cheaper, and in some ways more natural (*see* p. 45).

The Village is one of the parts of New York where streets are off-kilter (west of Sixth Avenue), so it can be confusing. There's plenty to see and do, with many galleries, cafés, restaurants and bars to choose from. The Village is an easy-going area with a relaxed attitude. You can live the way you like and it won't bother anyone in the least. Although basically a smart residential area, Greenwich Village still has a focus

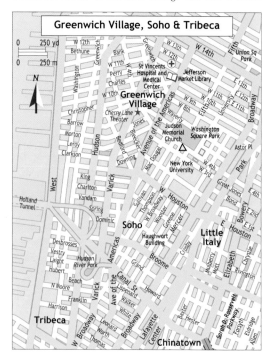

Greenwich Village, Soho & Tribeca

on creativity, and it can still trot out a few rather hardy eccentrics.

Artists are getting rarer in today's Village as prices of accommodation, particularly the space needed for big studios, have forced out the really creative people. Writers, needing less room, have clung on. The lovely old brownstones and brick 19th-century houses were homes to names such as Edgar Allan Poe and Henry James. Much harder to spot than painters or sculptors, today's writers still frequent the neighbourhood, and can be found in cafés, at lectures and even demonstrations. Poetry readings, literary events and book signings go on all over the place.

The Village is the place to find items such as unusual books, clothes and foodstuffs, and there are often stalls set up on quiet sidestreets to sell fascinating things such as carvings, candles and even cult objects. If you like shopping, there are lots of opportunities to find unique items here. If you wander up and down Eighth Street, the Avenue of the Americas (still known here as Sixth Avenue) and along such streets as **Christopher**, **Bleecker**, **Charles**, **Grove** and **Waverly Place**, you will get a feeling of this fascinating quarter.

Below: *Murals have become a city art form, such as this DKNY grey one on Sixth Avenue.*

Village Tour ★★
Head for Eighth Street to start. Greenwich Village is still full of that old creative urge even if it isn't old-style and impoverished any more. The architecture is rather eccentric but suits the bohemian air. The people can appear marvellously flamboyant. Crowds wander around after performances at the Cherry Lane, the Lucille Lortel, or the Provincetown Playhouse on MacDougal Street. All this makes a parade that is fun to watch.

CENTRE POINT

The business and shopping hub of the Village is where Eighth Street runs into Sixth Avenue. Here a major subway stop (West Fourth Street station) unloads visitors and locals alike, and there are lots of news, flower and hotdog stands. The Village is excellent for good food shops: many small specialist ones and groceries spill out onto the sidewalks and liquor stores rub doorways with smart shops and galleries. Looming above busy Greenwich Avenue and 10th Street is the clock tower of the Jefferson Market Courthouse. In the evening the place is livelier.

Below: *People chat, play chess and watch entertainers in Washington Square.*

Washington Square ★★★

Washington Square is set to one side of the Village, although it feels like the centre. This vibrant space is quintessential New York, whatever the season. Memories of great writers linger as kids play ball under the mature trees. The handsome stone arch which was completed in 1895 honours George Washington. The square also marks the beginning of Fifth Avenue and has been mentioned in literature. No. 16 is famed for being the setting for Henry James's novel *Washington Square*. Walk on the north side and you will catch glimpses of some fine façades. Some of them conceal apartments, such as no. 12, but no. 6 is a complete 1833 house.

Starting in the west you will find an area filled with students. They are the overflow from New York University (NYU) which extends for blocks around Washington Square. At the spacious **Astor Place** (with a notable subway station) there's a junk market and a modern sculpture of a big black cube. This is supposed to be movable so passers-by can interact and have a game with it. Here the liveliness of the area east of Washington Square is enhanced by various bookshops, some of them warrens, such as **The Strand** which is a vast, multi-million-volumed place at 12th Street and Broadway. There are many other shops, particularly along Fourth Avenue.

Note the **Judson Memorial Church** on the south side. This impressive Romanesque-style building is part of **New York University**, which clusters to the east of Washington Square. NYU students use the square as an impromptu campus, and figures hunch for what seems like an eternity over chess and board games. This is a good place to saunter and observe people.

Fifth Avenue still has some original houses and the westward streets have fine buildings and good shops. Walk along Bleecker, Bedford and Christopher Street, and look for MacDougal Alley and Patchin Place for its charm. Don't miss the beautiful **Jefferson Market Courthouse**, with its ornate features, on Greenwich Avenue at 10th Street. Voted the fifth most beautiful building in America, 'Old Jeff' is now a library.

The Hudson River Side

The West Village starts at the Hudson, which used to be a dreary area of truck stops and sleazy low-life bars. This dockside area is now completely renovated with attractions and facilities from running tracks to toilets. Piers are new and popular. The Hudson River Park adds greenery, while even the old meat-packing district has a new life. An unusual example of civic planning, the **Bell Telephone Laboratories**, became the artists' colony of **Westbeth**. This building was later redeveloped as apartments, yet without interior walls, so artists could have an open space or divide them as they wished.

The Gay Village ★★

It was here in 1969 that a confrontation between gay men and the New York police resulted in the **Stonewall Riots**, which are remembered as a milestone in the march towards gay liberation. The rioting incident led to the founding of the Gay Liberation Movement. In the Village haunts particularly they don't let you forget the fact that they've fought for and won their gay rights.

Most Village gay clubs, bars and shops are in the western sections, along and around **Christopher Street**. The street down to the river has been a gay highway but now more action may be found uptown in bookshops, bars and Lincoln Center. Places change so check local free sheets for new ones. Gay Village life still makes for an eye-opening stroll.

Above: *The Hudson River edges all of Manhattan and is often overlooked by tourists and, though rundown, is worthwhile.*

INTERESTED IN PICTURES?

Many artists here are weekend amateurs trying to rub canvases with the real artists. To find professionals who really strive for their art is not easy, but it is possible. In upper rooms and studios in the three areas they are at work and some do show what they do: check noticeboards and even lampposts for announcements. Alternatively, pick up a copy of the *Village Voice* freesheet from a bar or café. This way you may ascend a creaky stair and mix with the knowing who are finding out what the talent has to offer. Try to get to the twice-yearly Washington Square exhibition which is held outdoors in June and September.

Right: *In SoHo many
old-fashioned businesses
still exist, such as this
corner bookshop.*

SoHo ★★★

There was a time when SoHo (South of Houston) was
declining because the industry which had created the
district from the 19th century left it in empty desolation.
But it was being eyed speculatively by a new crowd.
Pushed out of Greenwich Village to the north by fast-rising
rents in the 1960s, artists commandeered studio space here
and squatted illegally, until eventually (and not untypically)
New York recognized the place as a new art zone.

Inevitably the area became fashionable, and smart
shops followed the lead of avant-garde galleries and
bought up the space fronting the cobblestoned streets.
The wondrously detailed cast-iron fronted buildings
(once thought, falsely, to be fireproof) suddenly gained
a new smart image and they were bought up, cleaned
and scoured and their high, wide interior spaces
opened up. Upper floors were rented out to the rich
and trendy, and the ground floors were revamped and
reborn as galleries and smart shops. New artists were
turned away and only those lucky enough to have
secured a space when the place was cheap, stayed on.

One of the first of these buildings was by James
Bogardus and was put up in 1848 on Washington
Street. SoHo is centred along West Broadway so branch
from this thoroughfare and discover Greene, Mercer

and Wooster Streets. The style is particularly prevalent in the Broadway area between the Canal-and-Houston section, and one of the best known and most admired is the 1856 **Haughwort Building** which was made for a china and glass business.

The reason why so many cast-iron façades rose up at this time was because they could be quickly erected on constructions supported by inner beams and walls. Iron façades also allowed for the economical reproduction of detail so dear to the taste of the mid-19th century – elaborate moulding was far too costly to effect in stone. Most of these mouldings were made and cast by Badger's Architectural Iron Works.

The fact that many of these buildings are swathed and webbed with fire escapes shouldn't detract from the beauty of the buildings. Before these fire escapes were made mandatory, many people died in fires when trapped on their upper floors. Fortunately the unattractive changes that many of these buildings later received on their ground and first floors are slowly being altered. The high, airy interiors also lend themselves well to showing examples of modern art – particularly large canvases and monumental sculpture – and their height (often six to eight floors) means a good number of residents can be accommodated.

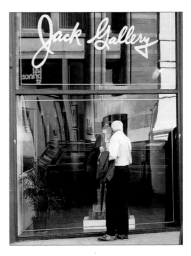

Above: *Sheets of glass, polished steel and modern art both indoors and out have changed SoHo.*
Below: *Small details on old buildings, often of a century ago, are fascinating to search out.*

CROSSING THE HUDSON

Oddly enough this isn't easy, though PATH operates under-river rail links. Take a bus across to **Weehawken** or **NY Commuter Ferries** and walk along the riverside roads, or simply go out on the **Staten Island Ferry**, which keeps Jersey City on its right going out. The best way to see Manhattan is from the Jersey approach to the **Lincoln Tunnel**, which gives a spectacular view of the Island.

WHERE NEXT?

You'd think that artists were fed up with being pushed from one quarter to another, and would all have gone to New Jersey. Some have; after all, it's just across the Hudson. But new arrivals now look to other derelict areas. Brooklyn, Williamsburg and DUMBO (down under Manhattan Bridge overpass) have already been taken over. Hoboken and Jersey City may be the newest art centres to visit.

Below: *A jumble of buildings, hoardings, fire escapes and parking lots make up the local streetscapes of TriBeCa.*

TriBeCa ★★

The selling off of SoHo to those with regular incomes able to pay much more for a slice of the area than the needy locals meant artists were on the move again. This time they migrated across the artery of **Canal Street** and southwest to the section they called **Triangle Below Canal Street**. Shortened to the convenient TriBeCa, it extends from this thoroughfare down to the edge of the **Financial District** and from the river to Broadway. West Chelsea and places beyond Manhattan are, however, the newest.

Unlike SoHo, the area has only recently experienced big changes, and retains a hard, gritty and industrial edge. It is therefore more genuinely an artists' quarter. Finance whiz kids, trendies and a few stars, such as Robert de Niro, have arrived to settle into lofts. Film studios, shops, galleries, even hotels and contemporary restaurants are established. It's certainly not rundown anymore.

The cast-iron buildings of this part of the city are, like those of SoHo, worth a tour all to themselves. If your interest is architecture, these 150-year-old structures are monumental, reflecting many Classical styles, and often are very beautiful in themselves. You will find many examples here and in neighbouring

SoHo, although many of this rich cache of cast-iron buildings are still unrestored. There's a movement by pressure groups to have the major streets made into landmark areas. Fine examples of cast-iron warehouse and commercial buildings can be found along **Broadway**, **White**, **Hudson**, **Duane** and **Harrison** streets. The streets are all named here, and the residents still frequent a few atmospheric old bars.

Visiting SoHo and TriBeCa Today

It's easy to wander these narrow canyon-like streets with guide book in hand, but why not sample the product? Watch out for notices of studio events and shows. Some are free while some charge a small fee for which you may get a glass of wine. You will see at first hand what the interiors of the buildings are like and how the real artists live and work.

Such open studio events are really for one thing – the artist wants to sell his or her work so perhaps you may find something you just can't live without. If art for you is merely dollars-on-the-wall and buying for future investment you'll be gambling so it is advisable to obtain inside information. A work of art, whatever the cost, is a souvenir of New York that nobody else will have!

Above: *A Harley Davidson in SoHo. All kinds of vehicles congregate on the streets of Lower Manhattan and motorbikes compete with the traffic.*

MOTHS TO THE FLAME

For many decades the city has been a powerful magnet for the arts. Every day dozens of young hopefuls from as far apart as Connecticut and California tumble off the bus or train, hoping to find fame and maybe money in Glitter City. For painter, writer, actor, singer, dancer or performance artist, New York offers the best possibilities of getting your act on. It'll be a hard path in such a tough city and just look at the competition – yet each arrival has stars in his or her eyes and the certainty that they are going to make it.

5
Chelsea and Gramercy Park

North of 14th Street and below Midtown is largely residential. The old established neighbourhoods of **Chelsea** and **Gramercy Park** are small oases carefully protected in a larger spread and, although undramatic, these often surprisingly quiet streets offer a number of simple urban pleasures.

For those with an eye for fine architectural detail rather than whole buildings, there is a lot to take in – from ornate doorways to stone friezes and sculpted figures on façades. To wander through the streets of Chelsea, a planned community, is to see the real residential New York and maybe encounter New Yorkers, who are very proud of living in the neat old houses of these sophisticated areas.

Throughout this area the great avenues run straight north and south, with the exception of angled Broadway. Marooned among a large amount of low-rise development are some surprising buildings. These are the early skyscrapers in the east 20s, not very tall in comparison with the nearby **Empire State Building** on 34th Street, but sensible, satisfying constructions with glinting gilding on roof and stonework. Among them is the newly cleaned **Flatiron Building**, one of the early skyscrapers to be built. It was originally called the **Fuller Building** but, owing to its unusual triangular shape, it became known as the Flatiron. Like so much of residential Manhattan, this is an intriguing mixture of buildings large and small, with much local interest if you are willing to take the time to search for it and see it.

DON'T MISS

*** Gramercy Park: a reminder of how old New York feels.
** Chelsea Hotel: a venerable hostelry for names in the arts.
* Madison Square Gardens: with a classic-style post office.
* Madison Square Park: surviving old buildings nearby.
* The Flatiron Building: one of the first skyscrapers.
* Union Square: a neat park on 14th Street with a farm market.

Opposite: *The Flatiron Building is on the corner of Broadway and Fifth Ave.*

Chelsea & Gramercy Park

SIGHTS TO SEE

Before 1811 New York had little planning, adding streets as the town expanded. Then it was decided to impose a practical plan on northerly development, so 14th Street is important as it marks the beginning of the grid system which was established in that year.

From the main cross street of 14th Street, getting around the town is simple – there's none of the oddly angled confusion of Lower Manhattan. All blocks are regular and all streets go directly north to south or east to west, with the exception of the old trail of Broadway and the thoroughfares running along the irregular edges of the island. The main avenues in the area are in general undistinguished; the important streets are 14th and 23rd, both wide two-lane thoroughfares with a variety of businesses, shops and plenty of life. For a walk, the eastern avenues (Lexington, Third and Second) offer more variety and interest, as they progress through contrasting neighbourhoods, while Broadway continuing from East 17th Street at the edge of Union Square has more interesting buildings and an uptown view.

Union Square ★

This used to be a dreary, rundown space where even the decrepit New York pigeons were wary. But New York values its green places, and there aren't many. Although not quite recaptured from some of its unattractive inhabitants it has been redesigned with handsome pavilions, newly cleaned up and planted, and it makes a welcome oasis and picnic place for workers. Its name

---

comes from the union of Park Avenue South, Broadway and 14th Street, not the fact that it was once the centre for the Socialist Party's May Day celebrations. Check for Christmas and 'green' produce markets.

The Early High Risers
It's hard to imagine New York without the skyscraper skyline as the city appeared in the 1920s. At that time the only tall buildings were clustered in this section – and they are still there, around Madison Square at 23rd Street.

Madison Square ★★
Just above Gramercy Park, where Madison Avenue begins, is a once undistinguished space at Broadway and 23rd. Before 1874 it was a cemetery and its 7 acres (2.8ha) are all that remain of a large area originally planned as a parade ground. Now a charming park, the trees make a soft frame for the classic old high risers and people often lunch here, enjoying the peace and quiet it has to offer.

The Flatiron Building ★
Although 22 floors doesn't seem much to us today, this building was a monster in 1902 when it loomed over Fifth Avenue. It was then the biggest skyscraper in New York! Built to conform to a triangular plot at the angle of Broadway and Fifth, this grand old New York survivor is a prestigious office tower, and is now protected from the wreckers as it has been designated a City Landmark.

Below: *Small green urban spaces, such as Madison Square, are much treasured in New York.*

TALLEST IN NEW YORK

Over the decades since the skyscrapers of New York City started to shoot up, several buildings have claimed to be the tallest in the world, only to lose the title to another even taller construction. The first of these was the **Flatiron**, then came the **Chrysler** in 1930, which was competing with the **Bank of Manhattan** and pipped it to the post by adding a surprise spire at the last minute. It was spiked by the **Empire State** a year later. This building held the coveted title for over 40 years. It is once again the tallest since the destruction of the **World Trade Towers**: they topped 1350ft (405m) but by 2012 the new Freedom Tower will be the city's (and possibly the world's) tallest skyscraper.

Below: *It's a marvellous clutter and unique, but don't expect the Chelsea to be a typical hotel!*

OLD RESIDENTIAL DISTRICTS

The two areas known as Chelsea and Gramercy Park are very attractive to New Yorkers and have some of the choicest and most valued properties beyond the pricey Upper East Side. These are areas not much visited by tourists, so if you want to get away from the herd, this is a good place to do it. There are no major sights, just a look at a New York that is old-style, refined and, as estate agents say, 'very desirable'.

Chelsea ★

Chelsea was developed by Clement Moore who wrote the festive poem *The Night Before Christmas*. Laid out in neat terraces of private houses, Chelsea was a model town of its time, stretching from 14th Street to 23rd and across to the Hudson. It is still known by the same name.

Much of the original work has gone, but one set of houses on 20th Street shows how the harmonious layout must have looked. This is **Cushman Row,** a row of fine brownstones, made more valuable because they face over an open space which is rare in Manhattan. It stands opposite the **Theological Seminary**, a large church with gardens. Walk a couple of blocks along Ninth Avenue and you reach the **London Terrace Apartments** – a New York legend on 22nd Street with their elaborate ceremonies. Chelsea is also home to several art galleries and the Chelsea Market.

The Chelsea Hotel ★★

This large hotel fronting 23rd Street between Seventh and Eighth Avenues is a place that has received many illustrious art lovers. Look at the commemorative plaques on the outside – names that extend from acclaimed authors to pop groups. It remains popular for visiting literary stars.

Gramercy Park ★★

Although the actual place that this name applies to is a small East Side garden square at the foot of Lexington Avenue between 20th and 21st Streets, Gramercy Park's name resounds far beyond the 60 dwellings located on the square. It is a very smart address to have. The buildings edging the square were designed by some of the best-known architects.

People living around the actual garden have keys to it. A century and a half after it was created, Gramercy Park is now the only private garden of its kind in the city.

Above: *The quiet and ordered enclave around Gramercy Park is often tourist-free.*

Theodore Roosevelt's Birthplace ★

Just off Broadway on East 20th Street, the President's birthplace is hardly imposing, being one of a row of brownstone buildings of 1840. No. 28 has five rooms reflecting the style of the President's childhood. His family moved when he was 15 years old. Open 09:00–17:00 Tuesday–Saturday.

The Players ★

A place to seek out here is the charming Players' Club, which is the city's principal club for theatre people. Special events (often for charity) are held here: it has a distinctive façade on east 20th Street. University and professional clubs are dotted around Midtown and several are notable. The Harvard Club at 27 West 44th has a floridly sculpted façade (the NYC Bar Association opposite is handsome Classical) and the Old Colony Club at 62nd and Park was the first women's club in the city. The University Club at 1 West 54th adds ornament to Fifth Avenue. Because university and professional clubs have influential and wealthy members, these buildings resist development.

ARCHITECTURAL REMNANTS

The loss of Penn Station, a grand building, was much mourned (today trains are under Madison Square Garden). Next to the lost original stands the old Classical post office, which may become the new train station. A century ago 6th Avenue up from 14th Street was *the* shopping street and you can still see remnants of the Classical Revival façades typical of the period, pillared and decorated with flowers and foliage. For craftsmanship, Gramercy Park and streets off Fifth Avenue show fine details in casting, carving, wrought iron and stone.

6
Midtown

Midtown is divided into Upper and Lower Midtown, with the halfway mark being the main thoroughfare of 42nd Street from the Hudson to the East River. Upper Midtown goes up to 59th Street where Central Park begins, while Lower Midtown covers the diverse area between 23rd and 42nd streets.

Clustered around the bright **Times Square** with its neon signs are the legendary showplaces of **Broadway** with enough theatre, cinema and allied attractions to keep you entertained for months! Great sights include many which are not to be missed: Park Avenue, the Empire State Building and the Chrysler Building, the Rockefeller Center, Grand Central Station, as well as the New York Public Library, the Chanin Building and the wonderful marble palazzo that is the Pierpont Morgan Library.

The one-time centre of Manhattan's shows, **42nd Street**, should be explored. Its theatres with the neighbouring West 40s have been renewed. Lower Midtown includes the Garment District in the west 30s and the many shops along West 34th Street. East is the district known as Murray Hill. **Fifth Avenue** and 34th Street are great shopping streets.

Midtown is the area most first-time visitors to the city will want to see initially, and maybe not leave at all, for most of Manhattan seems to be concentrated here in this middle belt of town. It certainly has some marvels on show and, one thing is certain, you won't be bored, though it would be a pity once you've tasted Midtown not to move out to explore other districts of the city.

DON'T MISS

*** Empire State Building: still a symbol of New York.
*** New York Public Library: famous New York institution.
*** Rockefeller Center: Art Deco glory.
** Chrysler Building: a monument to the car.
** Museum of Modern Art: a temple to the modernists.
** Times Square: simply the centre of town.
* Macy's: a shopper's heaven.

Opposite: *The Empire State Building is nearly 80 years old and it again dominates the skyline.*

THE GARMENT DISTRICT ★

New York is a fashion city, and that extends to the business of making clothes. It starts here, is promoted in glossy magazines, and what is designed and done here is news in the rest of the country. The west 30s around Seventh Avenue ('Fashion Avenue') are known as the Garment District and here in workrooms a great number of employees turn out ready-made clothes for shipment to points around the United States. Take a walk on any working day and you will see racks of clothes being swung out of workshops and warehouses into loading bays, bound for shops around the country. At 28th and Sixth Avenue is the Flower District. Visit early in the day.

Opposite: *You can't avoid seeing some of New York's famous buildings, and the Empire State often makes for a special photograph.*

Pennsylvania Station ★

New York classics are always under threat, and one of the greats, the old Pennsylvania Station, was a handsome Classical exercise in grand style and partially inspired by the Baths of Caracalla in Rome. It was pulled down in 1966 and is a sad architectural loss. It is still there as the city's main rail terminus, its Seventh Avenue entry marked by two stone eagles that once stood above its main entrance, but the station is now buried underground in the bowels of the **Madison Square Garden**. Even though this huge facility usefully hosts sports events, musical concerts and conventions, even circuses and commercial shows, and is a tourist draw, it is a sullen-looking edifice and architecturally sadly disappointing.

Across Eighth Avenue is the huge **Post Office** called the James A Farley Building. Its pillared grandeur once matched the vanished station. It, too, is scheduled for redevelopment – as an Amtrak railway station – but the developers have promised to keep the magnificent exterior untrammelled.

Empire State Building ***

This elegant building which still towers over 34th Street, contrasting with clusters of high buildings in Lower and Midtown, is a gem of Art Deco constructed during the Depression. Made famous as a landmark from the day it was completed, its steel frame enables it to stand at 1454ft (443m). It is often floodlit in colour and looks marvellous at sunset, sometimes with its head in the clouds, when light glints on its windows and metallic fittings.

You can ascend the tower to the observation platforms. Note the lavish Art Deco foyers and elevator banks before ascending to the platform on the 86th floor. From the observatory here you gain great views, and a trip up by express elevator is a Manhattan treat. Popular, but visit early or try a late night visit. Open 08:00–02:00 daily.

VP PARKS

Throughout Midtown you'll find small urban spaces that have not been built on and which have been turned into small gardens – or **Vest Pocket Parks**. These little oases, smartly designed, often with a café and maybe even a waterfall, can be found around Midtown and are sometimes the result of trade-offs over 'air rights' by local high-rise buildings. They make a welcome place to sit and relax in, especially on really hot days.

Below: *Visit Macy's – if shopping is your pleasure, you'll have fun here.*

SHOPPING ALONG WEST 34TH STREET

There are plenty of places to shop in this city from smart **Bloomingdale's** on upper Third Avenue to the popular Fifth Avenue stores, but the street many locals head for is still the favoured West 34th Street. This wide thoroughfare from Herald Square at Broadway to Eighth Avenue, is a hive of life with many shops and snack bars, its wide pavements crowded with shoppers seven days a week. One enormous store not to be missed is situated right at Broadway – **Macy's**.

Macy's ★

New York just wouldn't be New York without Macy's. In this gigantic block-long, nine floor-and-basement department store you do have everything. It claims to be the largest department store in the world and even publishes its own directory. It used to have famous price wars with the long-departed Gimbel's, but now the 140-year-old Macy's rules. If you aren't 'just looking' and can't find what you're after then consult the Visitors' Center which is situated on the mezzanine floor for information. You can also make bookings for restaurants and shows here. Macy's even provides a professional shoppers' service as well as an interpretation service.

Mid-West Side ★

At the other end of 34th Street on 11th Avenue is the vast **Jacob K. Javits Conference Center**, named after a New York senator and one of the reasons why the city is a big player in the conference and meeting business. On Eighth Avenue between 40th and 42nd is the **Port Authority Bus Terminal**, a large modern multi-level building where thousands of commuters come in every day. It also handles long-distance travel and since coach fares are cheap, it's very popular. It used to be an unpleasant place with a population of depressing down-and-outs but that has changed and it's now much more attractive with restaurants and coffee bars. The area behind it, from Ninth Avenue westwards, can be unsafe after dark.

Above: *The New York Public Library is a revered monument at 42nd and Fifth Avenue.*

New York Public Library ★★★

At one of the city's busiest intersections stands a grande dame of a building, the handsome Public Library. A popular meeting place is the flight of steps up to its impressive entry. It has a vast repository of documents, art, letters and books and there are frequent special exhibitions. The New York Public Library is a reference, and not a lending library (there are 80 branches around the city for that) but you are welcome to visit.

Built in stone in grandiose Beaux-Arts style the Library is as opulent within as without and has a vast entry hall. You ascend the baronial marble staircase to the vast Reading Room on the third floor. Be sure to ask about a free tour (11:00, 14:00 Tue–Sat, 14:00 Sun, meet at information desk) and remember to look out for the fountains and the pair of lions guarding the steps outside. Open Monday–Saturday. Opening hours vary. Closed Sunday.

THE BIG PARADE

Every November a big event hits New York and the TV screens across the entire country. It's the renowned Macy's Thanksgiving Day Parade when the store sponsors a huge procession of decorated floats, specially shaped helium balloons, crowds of costumed extras including cartoon characters, dancing and drumming bands and in the last float who do you think? Jolly old Santa Claus with his reindeer of course, to remind us all that at heart it's still a commercial event.

Right: *The UN Building occupies a large East River site and with its terraces and gardens it is a popular attraction for many visitors.*
Opposite: *The 1930s live on. Hidden during construction, the crowning needle was produced on completion of the Chrysler building.*

MURRAY HILL AND EAST 42ND STREET

Murray Hill is a largely residential area in the high 30s around Lexington and it is a pleasing area to explore. Around **Murray Hill** are several attractions, from the shops and bars of Third and Second avenues to a parade of striking buildings, many of them along East 42nd Street, which is well worth the long stroll.

Pierpont Morgan Library ★★

This immaculate, small Renaissance-style mansion of white marble containing a fabulous family collection is on East 36th Street. The Library, once home to the Morgan banking family, was built in 1904. This small, yet exquisite, collection was first opened to the public early in 1924 by the son, J Pierpont Morgan Junior. It has some quite extraordinary treasures within. In sober settings and ornate decors taken from European palaces this hoard of rare manuscripts, original music scores, precious stones and books – including a very rare Gutenberg Bible – is one of the most fascinating in the city. Open 10:30–17:00

Tuesday–Thursday, 10:30–21:00 Friday, 10:00–18:00 Saturday and 11:00–18:00 Sunday. Closed Monday, Thanksgiving Day, Christmas Day, and New Year's Day. www.themorgan.org

United Nations Building ★★

Over on 1st Avenue and East 44th Street, by the East River, rises a striking slab of glass and steel. It's the United Nations Building which is open every day and offers regular tours. This is the place to go and see how this organization functions. There are visits to the chambers where the General Assembly sits as well as visits to various other counsel chambers. Look out for the Leger paintings in the Assembly Hall and the Chagall windows in the foyer. For lunch the UN restaurant is formal, but it's worth eating there if only to see the river views. Outside, flags of member nations flutter and the gardens by the river make a memorable walk. You can obtain free tickets at the information desk for certain sessions. Open for tours 09:30–16:00 Mon–Fri, 10:00–16:30 Sat & Sun.

Chrysler Building ★★

A slender and impressive monument to **Art Deco**, much loved by New Yorkers, this famous skyscraper at Lexington and 42nd is the Chrysler Building. It was constructed as the New York headquarters and additionally as a praise-poem to the Chrysler motor car. It is 77 storeys high! This enduring monument to the motor car is appropriately adorned with all sorts of decorative elements from grilles and ornaments to hub caps, friezes of 1930s motor cars, and symbols of energy. These are particularly noticable at night when the sleek grey-blue Chrysler bursts into dazzling light. It's unique, yet a typical example of New York's wonderful sense of excess in high Art Deco. Not open to visit but go inside and see the lobbies and the interior fittings.

PROBLEM PEOPLE

New York is a big city and like so many other major urban centres it attracts all kinds of people. It's easy to fall through the net in Manhattan and be a dropout so you will find many beggars, panhandlers and down-and-outs here. They cluster in certain parts – the Bowery, around Eighth Avenue in certain sections, and at the waterside and some subways. Recently there has been an attempt to move them and so exploring the city has become easier. Most New Yorkers don't concern themselves about the fate of these sad people and are often only glad to see them dispersed.

CARNEGIE HALL

A revered concert hall in a high Victorian style, Carnegie Hall on West 57th Street is a place many artists are proud to play in. It's over a century old yet its acoustics are rated so highly that the New York Philharmonic is relocating here. Most nights have different attractions, ranging from soloists to small groups. After the concert you may catch a glimpse of the stars at nearby restaurants and bars along West 57th Street. www.carnegiehall.org

Grand Central Station ★★

There are more amazing buildings along the stretch of 42nd Street. Facing Park Avenue South and, effectively cutting the famous avenue in half, is the vast **Grand Central Station** with its façade of a magnificent array of statues around a big gilded clock. It's just as fanciful inside with throngs of commuters thrusting through high-ceilinged marble halls. One place you shouldn't miss is the **Oyster Bar** with its shell shape harking back to the grand days when Grand Central ran many more trains than it does today. Above the station is the giant **Met Life Building**, which irritates many New Yorkers because it dwarfs the station and cuts off the Park Avenue view.

Further along on the South side of 42nd Street is the 1930 **Daily News Building** in black slabs (note the huge rotating globe inside) and the handsome steel-and-glass atrium of the **Ford Foundation** at 43rd and Tudor City Place. This building has a garden caged in glass, 12 storeys high – great if you want to come out of the rain! The **Chanin Building** at 122 East 42nd Street is another Art Deco building of style with a lobby decorated in gilt and with unusually designed, graceful chandeliers.

Other notable buildings in the area include several churches. At Madison and 35th Street stands the **Church of the Incarnation**. Within are sculptures and Tiffany glass. The **Marble Collegiate Church** at Fifth Avenue and 29th Street has roots dating back to the Dutch occupation, but it's better known as the first church in America to have had an electric organ. At 25th and 5th, the **Church of the Transfiguration** is the home of New York's theatre folk – engagingly small, 'the little church around the corner' has the look of a country chapel, a certain fairytale charm in the city.

Below: *The very grand concourse of Grand Central Station.*

FIFTH AVENUE – WEST SIDE

Fifth Avenue offers many sights to the visitor. Its famous stores line the avenue in Midtown. Be sure to take a stroll from 34th up to 59th Street. There are a parade of shops from **Lord and Taylor's** to **Saks** and from **Tiffany's** to toyshops. You certainly won't be bored especially when the avenue changes like a kaleidoscope! Famous shops mingle with boutiques, as well as cut-price carpet stores and art and jewellery shops.

Best of all it's always busy with people, especially at the weekends and at festival times. Strolling along this part of Fifth Avenue you will truly feel that you are in the throbbing heart of a great metropolis.

Fifth Avenue is the dividing line for Midtown and one of New York's great walks. A major cross street, 57th, makes a marvellous walk especially if you like to window-shop – the galleries and boutiques of East 57th and uptown Madison Avenue are famous and often fabulous. At 59th, where Midtown ends, you arrive at Central Park South. This wide cross street is the southern border of Central Park with grand hotels such as the **Plaza**, the **Ritz-Carlton** and **Jumeirah Essex House** and glamorous restaurants offering wonderful views of the greenery just across the road. You can do the ultimate tourist thing here and rent a horse and carriage for a trot through the town and park. The apartment blocks here are most sought after because they face the park.

ANTIQUES

You might not think New York would be a place to find antiques, but this city thrives on auction sales, and serves up many surprises. There are antique marts with lots of stands here, fine for bargain hunting and browsing on a cold or damp day. Try the **Place des Antiquaires** at 125 East 57th, or not far off on Second Avenue, the **Manhattan Antique Center.**

TOY SHOPS

Don't even think of visiting a toy-palace like **FAO Schwarz** at 767 Fifth Avenue at Christmas time unless you like to inflict punishment on yourself. Not only is the place crammed, but there are queues or 'line-ups' out in the cold on 58th Street waiting to get in. Once in the place it is like a gigantic game, with salespeople dressed in costume and uniform demonstrating all the latest toys and fads. Take kids if you can, but just keep a hold on the credit cards if you don't want a big bill. This one's an expensive bazaar.

Below: *Times Square isn't a square, it's a confluence of roads. Once dilapidated and dangerous, it's been cleaned up in recent decades. New, lively and safe.*

Times Square ★★

It's still crowded and lit up with advertising signs but has nevertheless retained some kind of glamour. The square is actually a triangle extending from 42nd Street to 45th Street, the point at which Seventh Avenue crosses Broadway. There are many restaurants, bars and shops, and best of all the nearby theatres of Broadway which are a big lure to many visitors. Look for the half-price booth called TKTS at the top of the square for bargains. There is a Visitor Information Center, open daily from 08:00–20:00. *The New York Times*, the daily paper that gave the square its name, occupies a grim set of buildings on West 43rd Street. For many, Times Square is quite simply the centre of town.

Rockefeller Center ★★★

Between 47th and 52nd Streets off Fifth Avenue, this centre is one of New York's great pieces of urban planning. It has a set of stylish 1930s buildings, gardens and walks set in 29 acres (11.7ha) at the heart of Midtown, opposite St Patrick's Cathedral. The whole complex can take quite a long time to see but do at least walk down the main avenue with its glorious flowery gardens to the central sunken plaza – a great place for New York

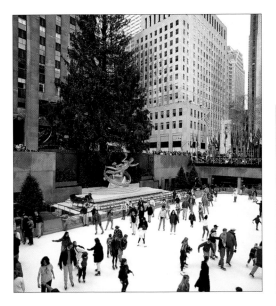

Left: *During the year there are always crowds at the Rockefeller Center, and in the winter there's skating.*

GETTING ON IN NEW YORK SOCIETY

The 19th-century coal and steel magnate Henry Clay Frick, a businessman lusting after social status, had his choice collection put together by Lord Duveen, the well-known art dealer. After the house was ready and receiving visitors in its marble halls, Frick was visited by a writer who gasped as she entered, 'My god, how Duveen!'

socializing! The plaza is an open-air restaurant in summer and in winter it becomes a skating rink under the looming statue of Prometheus. There are lots of stylish shops and do take note of the individual detailing of this rich monument to Art Deco in metalwork, tiles, glass and sculptured works.

At the rear of the Rockefeller Center, within the complex itself, is a mammoth theatre that is a New York institution: **Radio City Music Hall**. It was opened in December 1932 after having been lovingly restored. With almost 6000 seats, this is America's showplace, host to a range of attractions, especially when the big Christmas Spectacular has the legendary Rockettes high-kicking. At other times of the year it is host to a range of attractions. In style it is high Art Deco, with fabulous decors – even the men's toilet is in the period! If you can't find time to see a show then take a tour for a modest fee. They last an hour and give you a marvellous introduction to both front and backstage aspects of a great American theatre. www.radiocity.com

HELL'S KITCHEN

Though its picturesque name conjures up a descent into an inferno, this area of the west 40s and 50s over towards the Hudson is much tamer now. Once a quarter of poor new settlers and warren-like tenements, it's been improved and new residents have moved in. Like Eighth Avenue, it has been cleaned up and the armies of prostitutes and their glitzy pimps have withered away to the occasional solitary one. Also here around Broadway are the major theatres and a new restaurant area west of Eighth Avenue in the upper 40s which has added a touch of class to the area.

Right: *Sixth Avenue (or Avenue of the Americas) at the grand marquee of Radio City Music Hall.*

American Folk Art Museum ★★

Down the street from the MoMA building, and often overlooked as a result, is the newly housed American Folk Art Museum (at 45 West 53rd Street.) It was founded in 1956 by the American Craft Council, the building being specially designed for the purpose, and its permanent collection today contains thousands of craft artefacts – from teapots to chairs to baskets to rugs – on four storeys. Open 10:30–17:30 Tue–Thu, Sat, Sun, 10:30–19:30 Fri. The library next door has a distinguished collection of children's books.

Museum of Modern Art ★★★

This is often considered to be *the* temple of modern art, and for many it is one of the greatest shows in the city. It's welcomed return revealed to its many afficianados that the old building on West 53rd Street has been remodelled and expanded very stylishly, and with immense imagination. MoMA has all the great American artists, as well as famous Chagall, Mondrian and Picasso paintings. The museum has as its special preserve all modern arts from photography to film, paintings to prints, bibelots to books, as well as sculpture and architecture. Open 10:30–17:30 Mon, Wed, Thu, Sat, Sun, 10:30–20:00 Fri; www.moma.org

THEATRES

Broadway theatres are a big lure for tourists from all over the world. Seats can be expensive, but remember the low price ticket services around Times Square. Broadway offers you a taste of American culture and the good news is that theatres are busy again and new ones are being added. The once-dilapidated ones along 42nd Street have been beautifully restored, along with the street itself. Among the latest are the New Amsterdam and the American Airlines, and others will follow. Although large, many of the Broadway theatres have very limited foyer space.

Since it first opened in 1929, MoMA has been pleasing and shocking. Now that MoMA has returned to its Manhattan base, it is a great magnet again. If contemporary arts are your pleasure, you do not want to miss this place.

Classic Skyscrapers

The 40-year-old Seagram Building is one of the great beauties of Park Avenue; it houses the smart Four Seasons restaurant. The brownstone Villard Houses were important city residences of a century ago: now they abut the brassy glass tower of the Palace Hotel on Madison and house a smart and characterful hotel bar and the renowned Le Cirque restaurant. Here also are the offices and bookshop of the Municipal Art Society. Nearby, the 1924 Crown Building on 57th Street is faced on its upper levels with gold leaf. Other notable classic Art Deco buildings include the General Electric at 570 Lexington; the French building, bronze reliefs at ground floor, elaborate tiling on its tower at 45th and Fifth and the Fuller Building at 57th and Madison. Some of the buildings have gone out of their way to establish an eccentric style, such as the Chippendale chest effect on West 56th Street. New York City is always adding new buildings: soon the profile will be altered yet again with a new edifice on the site of the World Trade Center.

MUSEUMS

Most of the city's museums gained their treasures from private collections. The rich New Yorkers are often commemorated with the names of individual galleries or extensions to the buildings. However, aside from grand galleries, many small museums can easily go unremarked in the city. If you have a specialist interest ranging from dolls to railway memorabilia, chances are there is a collection for you.

Left: *The Museum of Modern Art, with a host of treasures, always has a stream of visitors. The renewed building is strikingly unusual and makes MoMA a leading NYC attraction again.*

Below: *Within the Waldorf-Astoria the public rooms are a gilded dream of Art Deco grandeur.*

FIFTH AVENUE – EAST SIDE

There are so many interesting sights in Midtown its hard to get them all in without resorting to a boring list. Many are central and are situated along Fifth Avenue, from the **Trump Tower** to the **Rockefeller Center**, but others are a bit off the track and worth searching for. Walk along the narrow Madison Avenue for a parade of old buildings bristling with decoration, though some only explode into the exotic at their summits.

Trump Tower ★

The **Trump Tower** on Fifth Avenue is eye-catching, a spectacular building with a corner of its glittering glass façade shaved off to allow a tumble of trees and vegetation to hang dramatically over the avenue. You can go in and explore its huge atrium and shops.

The Waldorf-Astoria ★

The truly grand be-flagged Waldorf-Astoria Hotel on Park Avenue at 49th Street didn't start off here, though it is now at a much more fashionable address than its original one. Before the Empire State was built, two cousins, Astor and Waldorf, had turned one-time family homes then on the site into two hotels. Moved uptown

Left: *Tall, pointed Gothic arches, magnificent rose windows and sculptured columns make St Patrick's interior impressive.*
Below: *St Pat's, as New Yorkers call this cathedral, viewed from the sculptures from the Rockefeller Center's mall.*

to make way for the new skyscraper, the cousins amalgamated the hotels which became the famous Waldorf-Astoria, a lush Art Deco palace that has hosted many of the greatest names of the 20th century.

St Patrick's Cathedral ★★★

A twin-spired 19th-century Gothic construction, St Patrick's Cathedral is the seat of the cardinal of New York and America's biggest Catholic cathedral, which is situated at the centre point of Fifth Avenue. Every year the Cathedral is the focus of the St Patrick's Day Parade. It's very much a centre of worship, its cool interior flickering with candles. Open 06:30–20:45 daily. Particularly noteworthy is the great rose window, designed by a 20th-century master of stained-glass design, Charles Connick.

7
Upper East Side

The Upper East Side is New York's class act; the place most New Yorkers would prefer as an address if they could afford it and if they could only find a decent spot to perch in. Some residents have been holed up here for decades, and aren't about to give up apartments that probably seemed expensive when they moved in and are now bargains. As you might expect, the neighbourhood is filled with handsome, usually clean streets, a range of pleasant places to eat, many small art galleries and the best and smartest shops.

The Upper East Side is an area that extends from East 59th Street up to the top of Central Park with Fifth Avenue and to East 96th Street where Spanish Harlem begins. Underneath the central mall from 42nd Street glide the railroad lines from Grand Central Station; they are discreetly covered over under Park Avenue's grassy central divide until they emerge at 94th Street.

The Upper East Side is bordered by the **East River** to one side and the great swathe of greenery to the west where **Central Park** ploughs its green patch among the high risers. It's New York's finest open space, its southern edge stretching from Fifth Avenue to Central Park West. The park borders one of the city's smartest thoroughfares: **Upper Fifth Avenue**, overlooking the park with a series of imposing apartment buildings for the most part with grand entrances and uniformed doormen. The area also has a distinctive European air with German and Middle Europeans in the north, while the Koreans and Vietnamese have opened up shops in the area.

Don't Miss

*** **Central Park:** New York's own green acreage, with a popular zoo.
*** **Metropolitan Museum of Art:** a spectacular art gallery.
*** **The Frick Collection:** great treasures in a sombre, grand setting.
** **Upper Madison Avenue:** New York's most exclusive stores – with prices to match.
** **The Whitney Museum:** modern masterpieces.

Opposite: *During the icy winters, skating in Central Park is popular.*

Upper East Side

Conservatory Garden
E 104th
Wards Island Park
W 96th
Central Park
Metropolitan Hospital
0   500 yd
0   500 m
Jewish E 96th Museum
Art Deco Eldorado Apartments
Guggenheim E 91st Museum
Gracie Mansion
Reservoir
Great Lawn
Metropolitan Museum of Art
Upper West Side
Delacorte Theater
Cleopatra's Needle
E 86th
Upper East Side
THE MARK
Whitney Museum of American Art
E 79th
American Museum of Natural History and Hayden Planetarium
Belvedere Castle
W 72nd
The Ramble
The Sheep Meadow
Frick Collection
Madison Ave.
Fifth Ave.
Park Ave.
E 72nd
Temple Emanu-El
Lincoln Center
RADISSON EMPIRE
Central Park Zoo
HELMSLEY
CARLTON HOUSE
E 63rd
E 59th
Queensboro Bridge
W 60th
Central Park S
Bloomingdale's
Hudson River
Broadway
Amsterdam
Columbus
Central Park West
West End
Henry Hudson Parkway
Riverside Dr.
Second Ave.
First Ave.
York Ave.
Third Ave.
Franklin D Roosevelt Drive
Roosevelt Island
East Channel
West Channel
East River
East River Drive
N

CENTRAL PARK ★★★

The park was first opted for purchase by the state as an open space in 1853 and a competition was launched for the design. It was won by Frederick Law Olmsted and Calvert Vaux, who converted nearly 850 acres (344ha) of wasteland into a wonderland. There are several lakes and ponds, and in the north is a reservoir circled by New York's foremost public running track. Although it is an urban park, with masses of statuary and such formal features as the **Bethesda Fountain** and terrace and the **Belvedere Castle**, there's lots of green space from the **Ramble** to the **Great Lawn** and **Sheep Meadow**. At the northern end is the formal **Conservatory Garden**. At 64th Street look for the newly revamped **Central Park Zoo**, which used to be free and rundown, but now they charge for its new look. There's a small collection of animals and a popular seal pool. Cars are banned at weekends.

Below: *Walking, jogging, cycling, skateboarding, or riding – the park attracts many activities.*

Very popular with plenty to do, in Central Park you can walk, jog, cycle or even ride; there's Shakespeare at the **Delacorte Theater** in summer and tennis on the courts near the reservoir. It's open all year round, but don't go at night, or wander around deserted places.

Upper Fifth Avenue **
The name Fifth Avenue is synonymous with smart New York and the wide cobbled sidewalk along the grand avenue reaches almost bucolic heights as it patrols Central Park. As you might expect, its name conjures up the image of the upper classes with their smart addresses. It's tree-shaded with its walks running by the low park wall, a fine place for a promenade or a place to take your expensive pooch.

Above: *Window displays on Fifth Avenue can be riveting, especially during Christmas when they vie for business with each other.*

Walk along the east side of the avenue: lined with exquisite apartments, yet a few of the grandiose residences that first claimed the turf a century ago still exist, and you almost expect to pay to breathe the air here, it's so exclusive.

Upper Madison Avenue **
Madison Avenue is narrower and more commercial, but paradise for those who like to window shop. The stores are often very expensive, specializing in particular things such as high fashion and interior decor items like antiques, Art Nouveau and Art Deco articles to Colonial furniture. The great auction houses can be visited, usually free, though you may need tickets to look at displays of coming auction items. Yet as this is New York there are still ordinary stores spliced in. Shopping is more straightforward along parallel **Lexington**, **Second** and **Third** avenues. Despite its name, **Park Avenue** is a dull boulevard with huge blocks of gloomy apartments.

> ### BUILDINGS IN CENTRAL PARK
>
> It's estimated that if all the constructions planned for Central Park by well-meaning (and some more commercially inclined) folk were built, the entire space between 59th Street and 110th would have been built over almost twice by now. Fortunately, there's a strong movement to keep the park green, but buildings that have elbowed in include the **Metropolitan Museum of Art**, the **Arsenal**, the **Zoo**, the **Delacorte Theater**, the **Tavern on the Green**, various stables, boat-houses and bandstands and a police station.

Right: *An old-style store with many departments, Bloomingdales is unique. It's expensive, but it is the place to find unusual gifts.*

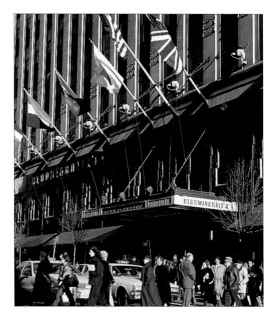

Bloomingdale's ★

Don't miss a visit to the favourite, expensive, and slightly eccentric store New Yorkers love at Lexington and 60th Street. '**Bloomies**' is the exotic showbiz store of New York and quite an institution. Fresh, trendy or fabulous, you'll find it here. Open 10:00–20:30 Mon–Fri, 10:00–19:00 Sat, 11:00–19:00 Sun.

MUSEUMS

Ranged along Fifth Avenue is **Museum Mile**. This is the home of the **Museo del Barrio**; the **National Academy of Design**; the **Cooper–Hewitt/National Design Museum**, housed within a handsome mansion on 91st Street; the **Jewish Museum** at 92nd Street; the **Museum of the City of New York**; the **International Center of Photography**; the **Goethe–Institut** and others. Off First Avenue in Carl Schurz Park is the mayor's residence, Gracie Mansion, which can be visited (on Wednesdays by appointment).

Solomon R Guggenheim Museum *

The Guggenheim at 88th Street is a controversial building (some people dislike it) which was designed by Frank Lloyd Wright and is his only building in New York. It is shaped like a flower pot and consists of descending ramps loaded with abstract and impressionist paintings by artists artists such as Picasso, Braque, Van Gogh and Chagall. Open 10:00–17:45 Saturday–Wednesday, 10:00–19:45 Friday (voluntary donation for last two hours on Fridays). www.guggenheim.org

The Metropolitan Museum of Art ***

This is one of the greatest repositories of art in the world. This palatial building on Fifth Avenue between 82nd and 86th streets should not be missed, whether you are fond of art or not. It's a showplace and a bit awe-inspiring; as you ascend the grand steps you have a real sense of occasion.

Like the Louvre or the British Museum, this is a star collection of major items, and you can only hope to see a part of it in a day's visit. It's absolutely huge: its many rooms encompass not just a great number of pictures but also sculpture, decorative arts and furniture, arms and armour, costume, and a whole range of antiquities. In addition there are regular exhibitions, some of them major retrospectives of particular artists or movements.

Below: *Frank Lloyd Wright liked to shock and his Guggenheim Museum is very controversial in its design.*

FOOD AND WINE

There are many fine restaurants on the East Side. Don't assume that when you see the label **American** tacked onto a restaurant description that it means hamburger, fries and coleslaw. Not any more. In many restaurants new chefs are creating wonderful, fresh ideas in US cooking. Although you can choose from a wide range of the world's best in New York, you may want to sample a few American wines. Many chefs will gladly introduce you to the 'local' wines and a surprise are the fast evolving New York State wines from the Finger Lakes. Wine producers are proliferating and they aren't all in sunny California: good bottles (particularly white) are also emerging from Washington State.

The American Wing is fabled, there are whole buildings from Ancient Egypt, an Assyrian lion, and rare and remarkable Vermeers. Van Gogh's *Irises* and *Cypresses* are here, too. Guided tours are available on request. There's a restaurant where you can snack or have a meal. Entry is by voluntary donations and you may give what you can afford, but it would be appreciated if you pay the full suggested amount, as this helps to cover the cost of special exhibitions, for which there is no additional charge or special ticketing. Open 09:30–17:30 Tuesday–Thursday (and Sunday), 09:30–21:00 Friday–Saturday.

The Frick Collection ★★★

This is a great star in the city's museum firmament and the kingly marble palace of a merchant baron is quite small – so it's possible to see it in a couple of hours. But it would be a pity not to linger before the marvellous paintings and lavish interior decors, with famous exhibits such as **Rembrandt's** *Polish Rider* and **Vermeer's** *Officer and the Laughing Girl* or **Gainsborough's** *Mall in St James's Park*, even if the building is rather rigid in style and feels a bit like a very luxurious funeral parlour! Open 10:00–18:00 Tuesday–Saturday (to 21:00 Friday); 13:00–18:00 Sunday. www.frick.org

Left: *Holbein's portrait of Sir Thomas More is just one of the Frick's gems.* **Opposite:** *The Metropolitan Museum's impressively spacious Sculpture Court is a place to sit and observe.*

Whitney Museum of American Art *

The Whitney Museum at 75th and Madison is uncompromisingly modern and filled with American art. The gift of Mrs Gertrude Vanderbilt Whitney, together with her large American collection, this museum is in a fiercely modern building. Look for work by Calder, Warhol, Pollock, De Kooning and O'Keeffe. Open 11:00–18:00 Wed, Thu, Sat, Sun, 13:00–21:00 Friday (voluntary donation last three hours on Fridays). www.whitney.org

Places of Worship *

You don't have to be Jewish to appreciate the grandeur of Temple Emanuel-El, the biggest synagogue in the United States seating 2500. You'll find it at Fifth Avenue and 65th. Also on the Upper East Side the onion domes of the Russian Orthodox Cathedral of St Nicholas adds a note of exoticism.

ACTIVITIES FOR CHILDREN

Visit the new-look **American Museum of Natural History** (Central Park West), with a parade of dinosaurs and lively programmes for children, or the **Hayden Planetarium** next door. Other options include the Bronx Zoo, the Brooklyn Museum or the Children's Museum of Manhattan. A harbour visit aboard the *Beast*, South Street Seaport's Lightship, and the four-masted *Peking* are also ideas. The Zoo and the Alice in Wonderland statue in Central Park or the Children's Garden and fountain at St John the Divine are good if it's a fine day.

8
Upper West Side

On the Upper West Side you are in a different world. It's the city's cultural suburb. Markedly removed from the Upper East Side across the park, it has its own way of life, attitudes and neighbourhoods that are more diverse and contrasted than almost anywhere else. You can find almost anything in the shops, and there's an overflow of movie houses, theatres, along with markets and museums. The Upper West Side is comfortable, unassuming and straightforward, and your true West Ender wouldn't live anywhere else.

From West 59th Street, **Broadway** cleaves its way right up the middle – it's the Upper West Side's main street, with the subway just under the grassed median. On either side, it is lined with roomy old apartment buildings that extend down its side streets. There are a few rows of private houses (off **Amsterdam Avenue** and **Central Park West** and dotted along West End Avenue) but mostly it's given over to apartments. These range from narrow buildings on cross streets to the vast, many-floored residences along Central Park West with desirable leafy views. In fact, Central Park West is a parade of such buildings of which the **Dakota** (New York's first luxury apartment house) is best known, and still an exclusive address.

There's the **Lincoln Center** and the **Juilliard School**, the **American Museum of Natural History**, **Riverside Park** and **Fordham University**. Although there's plenty to see and do, the real reason for a visit is to see a genuine New York neighbourhood at work and at play.

DON'T MISS

*** Lincoln Center: the city's cultural playground.
** American Museum of Natural History: the natural world in a recently renovated building.
** Hayden Planetarium: don't miss the astronomical shows.
** Riverside Park: fresh green turf by the Hudson.
* Central Park West: one of New York's stateliest thoroughfares.

Opposite: *Tall-towered Riverside Church, with an impressive carillon of bells, looms on the skyline.*

Upper West Side

[Map of Upper West Side showing Riverside Park, Henry Hudson Parkway, Riverside Dr., Soldiers and Sailors Monument, Broadway, West End, W 57th–W 96th streets, Lincoln Center, Beaumont Theater, Juilliard School of Music, John Jay College, Fordham, State Theater, NY Cultural Center, RADISSON EMPIRE, Columbus, HOTEL ARTISTES, ESSEX HOUSE, Strawberry Fields, The Lake, Dakota Apartments, New York Historical Society, Children's Museum of Manhattan, American Museum of Natural History, Central Park West, Columbus Apartments, Art Deco Eldorado Apartments, Central Park. Scale: 0–500 yd / 0–500 m]

CULTURAL VENUES

The Upper West Side is no longer a cheap area so the writers, actors and musicians who live here tend to be well off. They come here to work and to settle and to maybe bring up a family. Since the originally rundown area went through a programme of urban renewal and became attractive in the 1950s, it's gained a sort of cachet. Together with the cultural developments and university campuses like Fordham, it rapidly changed. Now along with the artists, white collar workers are also residents. The place is full of bookshops, art cinemas, smart shops and bars, new restaurants and theatres.

The Upper West Side's geographical spread of star sights is very much concentrated to the southeast, over to Central Park West. Many indeed are only a walk from the Park and spacious Lincoln Center or the green areas of Riverside Drive.

Lincoln Center ★★★

This grandly ambitious gesture on the part of the city brought music, opera, dance and theatre together on one plaza in a central location. The Metropolitan Opera left its old location in Midtown to an airy space and a new and bigger house here on 62nd and Broadway.

The **Metropolitan Opera's** ('the Met's') new premises opened in 1966 and it's one of the smartest places to be seen at. Standing right at the focus of the Lincoln Center plaza, its high white arches give glimpses of the grand red-carpeted staircase and

---

BOOKSHOPS IN THE CITY

New York has always been a book city with varied book shops, from grand stores such as the famous **Gotham Book Mart** near the Rockefeller Center to the multi-million volume **Strand** store in the East Village. The big firms have recently become even bigger. There are several along Broadway and these are veritable social centres, offering snack bars and sitting areas. They also stay open late at night and have become places to meet friends old and new.

the Chagall murals within. The oil company Texaco sponsors opera broadcasts played on national radio on Saturday afternoons as well as on BBC radio.

The Lincoln Center is regally flanked by **The New York State Theater**, home to the world-famous New York City Ballet and New York City Opera, and **Avery Fisher Hall**. Jazz is a regular attraction now. Drama is housed at the **Vivian Beaumont Theater**. Also here is the **Dorothy and Lewis B. Cullman Center** (**New York Public Library for the Performing Arts**), well worth a visit by theatre fans for its huge collection of theatre, dance, opera tapes, videos, manuscripts – and books.

The Lincoln Center is a handsome sight in pale marble grouped around a glimmering fountain. Between Avery Fisher Hall and the Juilliard are some modern sculptures, including a Henry Moore. www.lincolncenter.org

The Juilliard School of Music *

You can visit this school for professional musicians, singers and actors beside **Lincoln Center** for student performances, or recitals at the **Alice Tully Hall**. Some of America's best talents are nursed here. Aside from some of its alumni, it was briefly famous in the early 1970s when the great diva, Maria Callas, gave a short series of master-classes here.

Above: *The gleaming plaza and fountains of the Lincoln Center.*

Opposite: *The Met has more than 3000 seats for opera and ballet seasons.*

OPERA IN NEW YORK

From the early days New York had its own opera house. The first was on the East Side near 14th Street, the second in grandiose style rose in Midtown. Not big enough to hold scenery and costumes for a repertory that changes daily, it was pulled down and replaced by an office building. Now called Golda Meir Square, its ghostly presence is commemorated by a pavement plaque at Broadway and 38th Street. The Met in Lincoln Center is one of the few places where a rotating repertory brings different operas every night.

WALKING ON THE WEST SIDE

To discover the Upper West Side, it would be a good idea to take a long walk up Central Park West beside the park and admire the often fantastic architecture of the palatial blocks of residential apartments. No. 1 is the **Hotel des Artistes**, a site where many stars have lodged. Stop to look at the **Dakota Apartments**, where many famous residents have had their New York headquarters. The film *Rosemary's Baby* was set in the Dakota and in 1980 John Lennon died here. His wife Yoko Ono created **Strawberry Fields** in the park opposite in his memory. It is now known as the Peace Park. The Dakota name, legend has it, came from the time it was built, so far out of New York's centre that 'you might as well be in Dakota'. At 77th Street is the city's oldest museum, the **New-York Historical Society**, with paintings, silver and glass and special shows. www.nyhistory.org

American Museum of Natural History ★★

Below: *'Strawberry Fields' is a rare modern development in Central Park, and commemorates the work of John Lennon.*

Set on Central Park West between 77th and 79th Streets, the largest natural history museum in the world has been undergoing massive renovation and given a new look. There are fascinating new, state-of-the-art dinosaur halls, displays of animals living and extinct, ocean life,

birds and all sorts of stones from gems to meteorites. It's a great place, and there are interesting live programmes and films too. Open 10:00–17:45 daily; www.amnh.org

Hayden Planetarium ★★

Adjoining the Natural History Museum is the exciting new Frederick Phineas and Sandra Priest Rose Center for Earth and Space, containing what is still generally called the Hayden Planetarium at 81st Street, where you can see magical views of the heavens. Both museums are ideal for family visits; open 10:00–17:45 daily, shows 10:30–16:30 every half hour. The new AOL Time Warner Center has 'cultural space', shops and restaurants.

Note the shimmering Art Deco **Eldorado** apartments at 90th Street, then walk by the park to West 96th Street. This main street will take you to Broadway and the **Symphony Space** (headquarters for way-out new music). Continue on to the **Riverside Park** on the Hudson side.

Above: *Zabar's isn't just a famed Jewish delicatessen and bakery, it's a New York institution.*

Riverside Drive and Park ★★

This broad green area, hilly and wooded, stretches from 72nd to 145th Street and was designed by Frederic Law Olmsted, one of Central Park's creators.

Cross over on 86th Street, with its churches, in order to go down Broadway. The **Children's Museum of Manhattan** is on 83rd Street off Broadway. It is a fascinating experience for children, where they learn through play. There is a multimedia show and hi-tech equipment is available. Open Tue–Sun 10:00–17:00. Also, at various locations around here you will find all sorts of ethnic food and wine shops, as well as open fruit and vegetable stalls.

Small parks along Broadway commemorate the composer, Verdi (at 72nd) and the philosopher, Dante (at 63rd). The **American Bible Society** on West 62nd will appeal to those who are interested in the Good Book. If Art Deco fascinates you, then don't miss the sculpted façade of 1845 Broadway, which was once a garage and is now offices. Just down Broadway from here is **Columbus Circle**, where you will find exhibition halls and a cluster of big hotels. The Circle is also the gateway to the Upper West Side.

> ### West Side Eating
>
> Eating out poses no problems here, with a host of restaurants of all ethnic persuasions. But perhaps best of all is the array of shops offering tantalizing snacks and takeaway foods: from imported coffees to cakes there's everything here. Many offer Jewish specialities. The famous Zabar's has many kinds of bread, as well as delicatessen items and it's usually stuffed full with people buying their favourite, be it hard dark rye or zesty poppy seed rolls.

9
Harlem and Washington Heights

While Harlem's much-trumpeted Renaissance may have stalled, there is much of this stretch of Upper Manhattan that is worth seeing, especially for the discerning tourist and one interested in the history of the city. Harlem was the first stop for many blacks who were escaping slavery and persecution in the South. From the early years of this century they arrived from all over, and to this day continue to do so. Harlem can be slummy, rundown and terrifyingly poor, yet it conceals some surprising islands of wealth as well as several historic spots. President Clinton now maintains his office here.

The Harlem high street is **125th Street**, cutting right through the district and with all kinds of life and at all hours. East Harlem, from 110th Street up about 30 blocks, has been El Barrio, or **Spanish Harlem**, since Puerto Ricans began arriving here several decades ago. The best and safest way to see this area is to take a guided tour. These include visits to see choirs at gospel churches. All good Harlem restaurants will serve 'soul food'.

Columbia University occupies a site at the edge of Harlem from 114th to 121st streets. This is Ivy League New York, and its neighbour is **Barnard College**. At the edge of **Morningside Park** is the vast, unfinished **Cathedral of St John the Divine**.

North of Harlem, **Washington Heights** is now a great mixture of peoples and cultures. The **George Washington Bridge** spans the Hudson River here, and north along Fort Washington Avenue is the delightful **Fort Tryon Park** and the **Cloisters Museum**.

DON'T MISS

*** The Cloisters:** medieval marvels from the Metropolitan Museum.
** Cathedral of St John the Divine:** New York's mammoth Anglican cathedral.
* A tour of Harlem:** the best way to see black New York.
* Columbia University:** New York's Ivy League college.
* George Washington Bridge:** a huge yet delicate suspension bridge.

Opposite: *An extraordinary mixture, Harlem is a place where you can try soul food.*

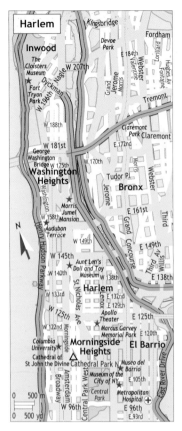

AROUND 125TH STREET

West Harlem has benefited in recent years from a much-needed injection of public and private investment. At its heart is the renovated central section of 125th Street. This continuously busy street is also named **Martin Luther King Jr Boulevard**, and handily there is an express subway stop here. Plenty of bars, clubs and fast-food spots. Here also is the famous **Apollo Theater**, alive and bright again and achieving a comeback; the **Studio Museum** and the **Harlem Third World Trade Center**. The one-time Teresa Hotel at Seventh Avenue and 125th was the site for Fidel Castro to address Harlem (unofficially) from a balcony.

For many escaping black slaves, Harlem was a promised land, a place to settle and live decently. This is still the dream of many residents of East Harlem, which contains some of the most socially deprived areas of the city. Here and in El Barrio (Spanish Harlem) reside more than half a million poor blacks and Puerto Ricans.

In the 1920s during Prohibition, Harlem was *the* place to visit, and music and song flourished at its clubs. The stars were there, and so were numerous jazz clubs and cabarets. **The Cotton Club** was the most famous, and with the **Apollo Theater**, it led the way. The Apollo has been refurbished and still presents popular talent nights – over the years it has launched many stars into the international firmament.

Although it's easy to get to 125th Street, many people don't like to visit Harlem alone. To see Harlem easily, take a tour with an experienced operator. This way you'll be comfortably transported to see places such as **Hamilton Grange**, the **Morris-Jumel Mansion**, **Striver's Row**, **Audubon Terrace**, **Boricua College** and the enchanting **Aunt Len's Doll and Toy Museum**, a collection of over 5000 dolls set up by a retired schoolteacher.

Spanish Harlem

This quarter runs from the northeast edge of Central Park above 110th Street and along to the East River (which at this point becomes the Harlem River). **El Barrio**, as it's called, or **The Neighbourhood**, is a place that resounds with noise and abounds with low-life. Its main stem is 116th Street, and there are many stalls and local foods to be sampled and savoured. Unfortunately it is a drug domain, so visit by day and take care. Don't stray off the main streets.

Museo del Barrio *

Below 110th Street it is safer and this is where, at Fifth Avenue and 104th, you will find the Museo del Barrio. This is a museum dedicated to the arts of Latin America and Puerto Rico and there is a changing and lively programme. There is also a permanent collection of interesting pre-Columbian artefacts. Open 11:00–17:00 Wednesday–Sunday.

Columbia University *

Founded in the 18th century, this is a member of the prestigious Ivy League colleges. It spreads between Amsterdam Avenue and Broadway from 114th Street. There are three undergraduate schools with over 18,000 students. The campus is essentially an urban

---

HARLEM'S HIGH TIME

They came from all over to perform at the Cotton Club. The music was blues and jazz, and the stars of the 1920s were Fats Waller, Jellyroll Morton, Billie Holiday, Charlie Parker, Bessie Smith, Charlie Mingus. The list goes on and on. Here, inventive music met memorable singers, and a new style was born. Wealthy New Yorkers came to hear the new music and to drink. During Prohibition and the Depression, Harlem certainly kept its spirits up.

HARLEM TOURS

To hear renowned Harlem gospel singing, take a tour. **Harlem Spirituals** at 690 Eighth Avenue, near Times Square, takes you by Gray Line, as does **Harlem Heritage** (tel: 212 280 7888) from the Gray Line depot at Eighth Avenue and 54th Street. This one also visits famous places, offering walking tours with gospel singing. For an old-style jazz night in Harlem clubs, go in a stretch limo with **New York City Limo Tours** (tel: 718 326 8866). The cars wait for you until well into the wee hours before heading back downtown. (Reservations necessary: 212 779 1122.)

Left: *A flower seller selling his wares in the cluttered streets and markets of Spanish Harlem.*

ACTIVITIES AT
THE CATHEDRAL

Aside from regular Anglican religious services, with notable music and choral works, St John's is also a cultural centre with a busy schedule of secular events, and there are bound to be theatre or dance performances and exhibitions when you visit. It's a lively place, and a concert here is a lovely experience. In the neighbouring **Children's Sculpture Garden** is a curious fountain and a display of works by local schoolchildren.

one, yet still spacious and with some handsome 19th-century buildings. Among them is the impressive Low Library, a few modern buildings as well as the colonnaded Butler Library. Nearby, Barnard College, beyond Broadway, is worth an exploratory walk. Tours can be arranged.

Cathedral of St John the Divine ★★★

Beside Morningside Park, this huge cathedral is situated at 112th Street and Amsterdam Avenue. It dominates the neighbourhood, and this Gothic edifice shouldn't be missed. As New York's Anglican cathedral, it is reputedly bigger than Notre Dame and Chartres and, although begun in 1892 and having survived changes of style, it's still not finished. There are several attractions within, from an ancient fossil to an altar dedicated to AIDS victims. Open 07:00–17:00, Monday–Sunday. www.stjohndivine.org

A fascinating place to visit on weekdays is the studio where the masons and sculptors work on the pieces needed to construct and decorate the building. The cathedral is being built on traditional lines and the masons can be seen at work in the **Stonecutting Yard** (Monday–Friday). Many works of art have been given to the Anglican cathedral and can be seen on a rotating basis in its museum.

WASHINGTON HEIGHTS

A huddle of apartment buildings and crowded streets, with many discount outlets and bargain stores, Washington Heights stretches north from 155th Street. This once-Irish enclave is now a great ethnic mix. It's also an area where you can taste unusual foods. Although it is becoming trendier, it still has a drug problem and, apart from cheap shopping, there's not much to tempt the tourist.

At 178th Street is the George Washington Bridge Bus Station and, in the shadow of the bridge itself, is **Fort Washington Park**, where a few remains of the original fort can be seen.

Left: Under the double decks of the George Washington Bridge is an historic fort and a landmark: the Little Red Lighthouse.

The Cloisters Museum ★★★

Fort Tryon Park is another of Frederick Law Olmsted's creations and has at its centrepiece old **Fort Tryon** which saw service in the War of Independence. But most famous is the museum, **The Cloisters**. Here, in elegant and cool surroundings, are medieval treasures from the Metropolitan Museum of Art. It's a wonderful collection and is easily reached by subway to 190th Street followed by a pleasant walk through the park. You can also take a direct bus from the Met itself on Fifth Avenue.

The building appears to be an authentic 13th-century edifice, but is actually comprised of bits of old French and Spanish monasteries. Open 09:30–17:15 Tuesday–Sunday (16:45 in winter). www.metmuseum.org

George Washington Bridge ★

Arching high over the Hudson River, this 14-lane, two-levelled suspension bridge crossing to the Jersey Heights is particularly impressive at night. From the Palisade Parkway on the other shore you get an equally good view, including Manhattan's lights.

WONDERS AT THE CLOISTERS

Here you can see a remarkable collection of medieval art from the Metropolitan Museum's overflowing vaults. The treasures range from illuminated manuscripts to the fabled Unicorn Tapestries. This is an experience not to be missed. In between the galleries are gardens containing sculptures, and the atmosphere is as calm and serene as the era it shows.

10
Beyond Manhattan

I nland and up and down the Eastern Seaboard there are many interesting places that will make an ideal day or half day out, be it a country tour, a trip to a beach, a theme park, or an historic town. Aside from the other four boroughs, all clustering close around Manhattan and which can be visited by bus or subway, the city has a wonderful range of parks and beaches of its own. Check with the tourist office or, if driving, follow local indications.

Other destinations offer many choices for days out by coach, self-drive car or train beyond the reach of local transport, into **New York State**, up into **Connecticut** or across into **New Jersey**. All three states have surprising countryside and tourist attractions of their own.

The Long Island Railroad will take you to the torpedo-shaped island that angles off Manhattan, its western 'toe' occupied by **Brooklyn** and **Queens**. Go further and **Long Island** gets really rural, with some of the most beautiful and wildest beaches and rugged and unspoilt countryside. Alternatively the Harlem Line from Grand Central goes to Connecticut, which has a long seashore. Also, beyond the commuter fringe and cluttered shore strip in the south, is very pretty wooded country.

There is a variety of things to do beyond the borders of the city and a wide range of places to visit, all within a short distance. The various tourist boards will happily assist you. Be sure to ask about bargain day-out fares as well as the special offers on coaches.

DON'T MISS

*** Bronx Zoo: with the Botanical Gardens – a real New York surprise.
** Circle Line and New York Waterway cruises: the best way to see the city from the water.
** Long Island: New York's seaside and country.
** Hudson River Valley: a day trip for scenic beauty.
** Staten Island: once off the ferry, a place for discovery.
* Princeton, New Jersey: a charming university town.

Opposite: *A handsome Colonial house with pillars and porticoes at Renselaerville.*

OLDEST HOUSE IN NEW YORK

Peter Stuyvesant or 'Peg Leg Pete' as he was known was not very tolerant of the Quakers and their religion. He acted very harshly towards them but they persevered with John Bowne as their defending hero. John demanded and received toleration of religions in the then-Dutch controlled colony thus laying the foundations of religious freedom for the future United States. His house, with some original furniture, is on Bowne Street. This simple, low building is the oldest home in the city and dates back to 1661. It is open to the public in the afternoons except Mondays.

Opposite: *The Queens' Dockland, East River, is a cluttered part of the inlet leading to Harlem River.*

BROOKLYN AND QUEENS

A cursory glance might not reveal much of interest in the two boroughs that lie side by side on the end of Long Island. The only bit of **Brooklyn** and **Queens** many people see is the drive in from **Kennedy Airport** and much of it is suburban sprawl. But don't dismiss it as worthless views of endless huddled housing interspersed with the occasional park. There are some surprising things to discover, particularly in Brooklyn.

Brooklyn was once its own city with a good deal of civic pride. If it had not been absorbed into **Greater New York** in 1898, it would now be one of the biggest cities in the United States. This is evidenced by its many civic attractions, concert halls and seats of learning, the grandiose buildings at its centre and by still-smart suburbs such as **Brooklyn Heights**. There's a sense of history too – the colony on the bluff was founded by the Dutch 350 years ago. They named it *Breuckelen* and, except for a dip into decline in the 1950s, it has remained a delightful place to live and visit. With its handsome terrace houses and harbour views, Brooklyn Heights is now a designated Historic District.

You can easily reach the Heights on its cliffs by subway, downtown bridges or through the 2 mile-long (4km) **Brooklyn Battery Tunnel**, the longest road tunnel in the country.

Beyond Manhattan

Brooklyn Museum ★★

Consider also a visit to this museum, a treasure house and one of the biggest museums in the entire country, with large collections of primitive artefacts of American Indian, African and Pacific arts. There's a fascinating hoard of things to see, from 18th-century colonial furniture and European paintings to Egyptology and ancient Assyrian sculpture.

There's also a mock-up of a 17th-century Dutch house with authentic furnishings, a costume centre and works by local artists of the Hudson River School. Open 10:00–17:00 Wed–Fri , 11:00–18:00 Sat and Sun.

The museum is at the **Brooklyn Botanic Garden** on eastern Parkway. Although small it has specialist gardens, collections and large conservatories. The borough houses the **New York Aquarium** and the remarkable **Brooklyn Academy**. Lots of lively theatre and dance at this grand Victorian theatre with additional smaller stages.

Brooklyn may have more people, but **Queens** is larger. It's gained new attractions such as the **Isamu Noguchi Museum**: a building vacated by the **Museum of Modern Art** should show works now in storage. **Public School 1** has been recycled for a gallery, **Queens Museum of Art** and the **Museum of the Moving Image** have moved in. Easy subway access. In sports Queens has the **USTA National Tennis Complex**, **Shea Stadium** and **Aqueduct Race Track**. Two of three airports are here, **LaGuardia** and **Kennedy**, while Newark is in New Jersey.

Brooklyn Academy

This big complex of theatres and galleries offers much that is new and contemporary to discerning audiences from all over New York. It offers leading international performers and companies, and is easy to get to from Manhattan – the subway station is close to the Brooklyn Academy.

NEW YORK TRANSIT MUSEUM

Housed in a historic 1936 IND subway station in Brooklyn Heights, and easily accessible by subway, the New York Transit Museum is the largest museum in the United States devoted to urban public transportation history, and one of the premier institutions of its kind in the world.

The Museum explores the development of the greater New York metropolitan region through the presentation of exhibitions, tours, educational programs and workshops dealing with the cultural, social and technological history of public transportation.

Go to www.mta.info for details of current exhibits and programs, or to shop the Museum's online store.

New York Transit Museum
Corner of Boerum Place
and Schermerhorn Street
Brooklyn Heights
212-878-1016

Gallery Annex & Store
Grand Central Terminal
Shuttle Passage, Main
Concourse
212-878-1016

Below: *Yankee Stadium, home to the New York Yankees for 85 years, finally closed its doors in 2008.*

THE BRONX AND STATEN ISLAND

Amidst the grimness of the Bronx is the **Bronx Botanical Garden** and the **Zoo** – a wondrous place indeed. This contiguous spread of 500 acres (202ha) is easily reached by subway to Pelham Parkway. Note that while the two are neighbours, entrances are separate and far apart. Near them lies Arthur Avenue – the city's new Little Italy.

Yankee Stadium *

Both the city's top baseball teams, the Mets and the New York Yankeess, will be moving to new stadiums in 2009. For more information (including ticket sales) contact http://mets.mlb.com and www.MLB.com/NYYankees The baseball season extends from April–October – only major matches are sell-outs.

Bronx Zoo and Wildlife Conservation Society ***

This is a winner; a century old, yet kept well up to date with several thousand animals, reptiles and birds, shown in large spaces that are made to be as natural as possible. All six continents are represented. There's a World of Darkness show for nocturnal animals and a children's zoo. Open Mon–Fri 10:00–17:00, Sat and Sun 10:00–17:30. Some exhibits are closed in winter.

Next door and to the north is the **New York Botanical Gardens** with azaleas, rhododendrons and many native American plants and trees. The Enid A Haupt Conservatory contains tropical plants. Best times for visiting are early spring through summer. Open 10:00–18:00 Tuesday–Sunday. www.nybg.com

Van Cortland House Museum *

A visit to a country house in the Bronx sounds a bit strange, yet here in the midst of it off 242nd Street is the **Van Cortland House Museum**. Unpretentious, it still stands in its park, now mostly put to use as play-

Left: *In the Richmond Settlement on Staten Island you feel as if you're in a country town.*

ing fields. This 18th-century country house was a head-quarters for General Washington during the struggle for independence. Although its name suggests a Dutch origin, it's really a simple Georgian stone mansion. Recently restored in its protected setting, it has a fine collection of period china and furniture and a few rooms are open to the public. Open 10:00–15:00 Tuesday–Friday, 11:00–16:00 Saturday and Sunday.

Staten Island ★★

Your journeys of discovery round New York don't have to be exclusively on the road or the underground. You can go by boat and anyway you can only get to Staten Island from Manhattan by ferry. And what a trip! If the weather is fine you can spend half a day or more on Staten Island and take the ferry from the Battery in Lower Manhattan. The journey across the harbour adds considerably to the fun. Staten Island is part of **Richmond**, a surprisingly large borough offering views of Lower Manhattan, Ellis Island and the Statue of Liberty and an introduction to the city's busy harbour as well. Here you can find several interesting things to see, including **Historic Richmond Town** (a restored example of an early New York village), the historic **Snug Harbour Cultural Center** and the **Jacques Marchais Center of Tibetan Art.**

CRUISING AROUND THE CITY

Aside from the famous ferry, you can make the best of fine weather by taking regular cruises to discover, or circum-navigate, Manhattan Island, or simply enjoy an evening of dancing and drinking. New York is a city on the water and outings go from several points. The **Circle Line Cruises** depart from berths at Pier 83, West 42nd Street. If you would like a more formal trip with dinner, there's the **World Yacht** which goes from Pier 81 and gives a lunch, brunch or dinner excursion. From Lower Manhattan's Pier 16 you can sail the harbour on **Seaport Liberty Cruises.** This one sails regularly from South Street Seaport in Lower Manhattan, and most will have live musical entertainment.

Above: *Where the wealthy play – yachts in the Sound off Long Island.*
Opposite: *Fire Island is a line of sand protecting Long Island from the Atlantic Ocean. There are superb beaches here.*

LONG ISLAND COUNTRY

Inland Long Island is often overlooked, yet its country pleasures are delightful. Rural roads, sea views, little restaurants offering local seafood such as the delicious tiny Bay Scallops. Try them broiled in butter. Small farms grow potatoes, corn and vegetables; there are lots of roadside stands in season to sell you fresh produce for picnics. You'll find plenty of quiet places for alfresco meals too.

LONG ISLAND ★★

New York is a marvellous place for a holiday but don't forget that the city, with its complex web of transport, both local and long distance, is also perfect as a base for the discovery of other cities, out-of-town sites and local centres of attraction. Long Island is a case in point. This huge piece of land, 120 miles (193km) long, parallels Connecticut's coast and extends into the Atlantic. It is essentially rural once you leave the New York suburbs. Trains depart from **Pennsylvania Station** (also known as Penn Station) but can be crowded at certain times of the day because they serve so many commuters.

You'll discover an undulating landscape that becomes ever more countrified as you go further north-east, with small settlements and neat farms. Trains are slow and the carriages are hardly modern, yet you get the best view this way: if you drive a hire-car you may find it hard to navigate on the elevated highways. Many Long Island resorts are accessed by jitney buses from New York City.

The **Long Island Railroad** will give you a real taste of the island, from pastures to open sea. Especially popular in summer, it will also take you to a number of resorts along the east coast as well as commuter suburbs.

BEACHES

There are beaches all around the island, but those facing the open sea are peerless wide stretches of white sand. Lapped by the Atlantic, with long, cleansing rollers, the shore is a perfect destination even out of season, but wonderful on a hot summer day. At weekends, though, the parks and beaches may be very crowded with New Yorkers bent on escaping the city heat. It's a good idea to take a picnic and to use the barbecue facilities offered in the state parks. There are many of these facilities and they are free.

The train stops at ferry points for the thin spit of sandy land known as **Fire Island**, a very popular destination in summer, dotted with resorts for every taste. The 40-odd summer settlements are connected by walkways and cater for families, singles and gay people. Fire Island is a long sandbar protecting the east coast of the island, home to small parks and a chain of seaside resorts and the beaches are wide and clean.

About two hours along the coast are the resorts known as **The Hamptons** – the neat little towns of Westhampton, South and Easthampton, the latter pair wildly chic in summer, expensive and filled with New Yorkers on vacation. It's as if the entire Upper East Side had flown out like exotic birds to perch here in cool summer cottages. You can continue further to the remote end of Long Island and **Amagansett**, which is where the rich and the less flamboyant have summer houses to get away from it all. The sands are wide, the sky and sea views huge and the beaches are often deserted. If you want an experience of peace then it is advisable to come out of season.

CONEY ISLAND

Once a lively amusement park, Coney Island has seen better times. Now it is a sad shadow of its former great days and many guide books don't even mention it. It sits at the end of a subway line on a wide, polluted beach yet it still offers fairground lures. Here, you'll find the New York Aquarium, Little Russia with its shops and cafés at Brighton Beach, and also a New York label for hot dogs – Nathan's Famous – where you must take the family for American frankfurters and fries.

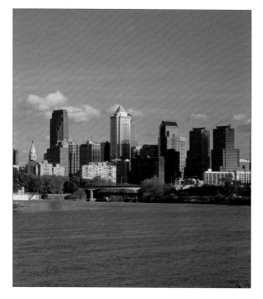

Above: *Philadelphia is just a bus ride away from New York City.*

NEW JERSEY

To the west is New Jersey, now being settled by New Yorkers especially near fast PATH connections. From the bluffs of the Hudson River just across the George Washington Bridge you get fine views of Manhattan from the Palisade's Parkway. Newark, much improved, has a good museum and shiny black office buildings rise over Mulberry Fishmarket.

Princeton *

An hour's train journey will take you to Princeton, another Ivy League university which is highly recommended for a day trip. This elegant small university town's campus is all in approved stone Gothic style. Friendly and photogenic, there are pretty white-fenced streets and clapboard houses.

Even the rich repository of arts and architecture and the city of Brotherly Love, **Philadelphia**, in the state of Pennsylvania, is only a 90-minute bus journey away.

Depressingly ugly Hoboken, Jersey City and Elizabeth may be, with their heavy industry and run-down houses, but they are not typical. Get beyond them and you will find pretty countryside and in the west, some smart 'hunting country'. With its northern towns very much sleeper suburbs for New York, its southern extremities very rural and even empty, New Jersey is a state of contrasts.

It has some very fine country but you'll need to allow time to discover it. In the far west is the lovely **Delaware Water Gap** along the wide river valley – drive and enjoy the small settlements and wonderful old inns on the Delaware banks, and New Jersey towns like **Flemington** and **Lambertville**. At this town you can cross into Pennsylvania and the town of **New Hope** which is the centre for the beautifully rustic Bucks County.

Atlantic City *

The sea coast of New Jersey, with wild country and wonderful extensive beaches, is a world away from Long Island, although in its long sweep from New York's harbour to the lonely country of **Cape May**, it has attractive seaside communities. The major one gained immense favour in the early part of the 20th century as a getaway place for New Yorkers. This is Atlantic City, with its famous attractions and sandy beaches.

Atlantic City reached a high-water mark in the 1920s (evoked in the musical *42nd Street*), but since then has declined in fashion. It's had its great moments, and continues to host major meetings and the occasional big party conference. The city still has the usual seaside attractions plus casinos. It sports some lures such as the famous wooden boardwalk that runs along the promenade above the beach and was the place to be seen 75 years ago when Atlantic City was smart and popular. The town has had to revamp itself, but its old hotels have character and charm.

THE PORT AUTHORITY BUS TERMINAL

A very important link for coach and bus travel, the terminal is a 24-hour operation and the Eighth Ave subway goes to the Kennedy connection, AirTrain. You can cross America from here – or take coaches to the three city airports. Clean, well-ordered and safe, it has good cafés and bars. Tel: 212 564 8484.

Below: *Atlantic City is now famed for its casinos.*

INDIAN CONNECTIONS

An Indian place name (Quinnehtuqut) was the original name of the river cutting through the state of Connecticut. There are many other examples of Indian place names in the state, some attached to scenic attractions, such as the Shepaug River Gorge, Lake Waramaug and the Housatonic River. The name Washington isn't Indian of course, but in the town is a collection of Indian archaeology and a replica of a Native American village.

Below: *Litchfield, Connecticut, is a quiet place and here you will see typical wooded country houses.*

CONNECTICUT

A little further to the north from New York, is **New England**. This area of six states has much to offer and two of them are within easy reach of New York. The most southerly of the six is Connecticut.

You can get to **New Haven** by bus or train. It's a comfortable town which was first laid out in the 17th century. New Haven has fine museums and three early churches at its centre. It is also the home of **Yale**, another member of the Ivy League club, and guided tours leave from Phelps Gate. You could visit the state capital, **Hartford**, which has a handsome state capitol building and connections with the 19th-century novelists Mark Twain and Harriet Beecher-Stowe. You can even go as far as Providence to discover the state of **Rhode Island** and **Newport** with its palatial summer houses built for the New York rich with the French chateau in mind. These destinations would be served better with a night's stopover in order to avoid having a frustratingly short stay.

Connecticut itself has a string of beaches along its ocean shore. If you can get as far as **Mystic** you'll discover an old whaling station and a maritime museum where craftsmen display old sea-going skills. Nearby **New London** is a lively place with a deep harbour and associations with the writer Eugene O'Neill.

Connecticut is also very rural once you have got over its southern commuter belt. It has small farms and old-style towns and villages. Some are typically New England with quite a different character in its residents. If you only have time for one or two then consider **Litchfield** or **Wethersfield**, both with a wealth of Colonial houses.

Left: *Along the Hudson River little streams join the broad river in its stately valley.*
Overleaf: *It is hard to imagine that the South Street Seaport once dominated the river. Now the Financial District dwarfs it.*

LOWER NEW YORK STATE

New York is actually a huge state with many attractions, but such lures as **Lake Champlain**, the **Finger Lakes**, **Rochester** and the **Ontario shore** are too far for day trips. The southern part of the state has much to offer, though, and it's charmingly low-key and agreeable.

A drive along the **Hudson River Valley** from New York has many pleasures and a host of small state and historic parks to visit. Stop at **West Point Military Academy**, for its museum and visitor centre, or scan the views from **Bear Mountain**. Stately homes, American style, are the **Vanderbilt Mansion**, **Mills Mansion** and **Hyde Park**, the Springwood estate of Franklin D Roosevelt. These beautiful homes are to be found in the neighbourhood of **Poughkeepsie**, once the state capital. At the present state capital of **Albany** there's much to take in too. Another beautifully rural drive can be followed through the **Catskill Mountains**, where Washington Irving's fictional character Rip Van Winkle fell asleep.

AMTRAK DELIGHTS

Want to skip the hire car? A day out by train from Penn Station is a special pleasure. You can actually take a very comfortable train trip all the way to Buffalo, with frequent stops along the way, especially along the Hudson Valley, if you are planning a slower exploration of New York State. A good idea is to take day jaunts to historic sites and riverside towns along the Hudson River. Lovely views extend all the way to Albany. Amtrak offers special fares, friendly service, and there's a café on board.

New York City At a Glance

Most times of the year, except in high summer (July and August) when it's often hot and uncomfortably humid, but hotel rooms are a bargain. In winter it can be sharply cold and frosty, but dry. As New York is on the same latitude as Spain, dusk does not come too early. Best periods are from **April –June** (spring) when the weather is balmy and **September– October** when autumn weather is crisp yet warm. Families celebrate during Thanksgiving (end of November) and Christmas (when you may get consider-able snowfalls) but New York makes up for it by being festive and fun.

New York is one of the best connected cities in the world. It's served by most airlines from all major world cities, often with direct flights. There is a choice of three airports and, while **JF Kennedy** and **Newark** handle most of the international flights, **LaGuardia** is usually for domestic services. You can also arrive by ship on occasional trans-Atlantic sailings direct to the West Side docks from Europe, notably the QE2 and the new Queen Mary. There are services by train from the US cities that still have rail connections. **Greyhound** bus

and other coach companies depart for all US and Canadian points, and some Mexican ones too. If you plan to see New York City as part of an Eastern Seaboard tour you can rent **cars** easily from a big selection of rental agencies in town and at all airports. You may be charged a fee to drop them off at a different destination from the pickup point. Take out full insurance. Gas (petrol) is very cheap.

There is a very good public transport system, although some people are put off at the thought of descending into the **subway**. Don't be. The subway is safe except late at night when it's less used. It's been cleaned up, and well-policed over recent years. It runs for 24 hours, it's efficient, cheap and very fast, especially between express stops. The subway extends all over the city except Richmond (Staten Island) and New Jersey. A separate system called **PATH** brings commuters in under the Hudson from Jersey City.

The **subway map**, obtain-able at every station or from information booths, is a bit confusing for visitors and you may need help in working out which train to take and where you get off and transfer. Buy cards for varying amounts of the flat price fare

all over the centre at subway booths. These can also be used on buses, which operate principally along main avenues. These can be slow at rush hour. The Metrocard, a magnetic farecard, is stan-dard for use on subways and, within New York City, on all public and most private buses, with a free transfer between subway and buses. Private coach services link the airports to the **Port Authority Bus Terminal** on Eighth Avenue, or the 42nd Street entrance of **Grand Central Terminal**. The subway (Eighth Avenue A Express train, same as the city flat fare) also links Kennedy Airport with a new **AirTrain service** ($5) that encircles and connects with all terminals and parking lots.

Taxis: Yellow cabs are to be hailed anywhere at any time, and they are frequent and reasonable. You can rent **bicycles** at certain points (a good way to encompass Central Park) and some younger visitors even glide around town on **skates** or **rollerblades**. **Walking** is also easy and direct, since almost all streets go from east to west and avenues from north to south, and it's certainly safe on busy main roads in central Manhattan.

Suburban Trains: Port Authority Trans-Hudson (PATH) operates 4 lines to and from New Jersey with

New York City At a Glance

connections at Hoboken and Newark to NJ Transit. Information toll-free, tel: 1 800 234 7284. Metro-North goes from Grand Central to the northern suburbs and Connecticut, tel: (212) 352-4900. The **Long Island Railroad** goes to the island from Pennsylvania Station, tel: 1 718 217. **Penn Station** also serves with Amtrak cities beyond New York that have rail connections. Information from the **Metropolitan Transit Authority**, tel: 718 330 1234, 24 hour daily service.

WHERE TO STAY

Many possibilities exist in a range of prices, from **hostels** and **bed-and-breakfasts** to **motels** and top luxury hotels. It's unlikely that most visitors will want to stay anywhere other than in the centre, so the following are almost all Manhattan-based sugges-tions, and since there are so many, this is only a short representative list of possi-bilities. More detailed lists can be found at **CitySearch,** www.newyork.citysearch.com or www.NYTAB.com for occasional deals. Booking services: try the recommended **Express Reservations** at www.quikbook.com tel: 212 779 7666 (outside the US) and 800 779 7666 (inside), or **Accommodations Express**, tel: (800) 444-7666, a seven-

day-a-week free service offering room discounts. On weekend visits you will find that many **hotels** will com-pete to offer lower rates when business people have gone home. Check newspa-pers or the **NY Convention and Visitors' Bureau** (810 Seventh Avenue, NY 10019) for bargain weekend pack-ages, or ask hotels when booking direct. Packages can also include tours, free meals, plus all those little extra luxuries to invite you in to fill rooms at quiet times. Bear in mind that the price quoted will not usually include the steep local NYC taxes. These may well add 13–25% plus $2 to your bill. Note that Manhattan telephone numbers are all prefixed 212 or 646, if calling long distance, but beyond the island they differ. Another option is **Homestay New York**, a well-respected accommodation service for those who want the experience of living with real New Yorkers. Hosts are carefully screened and matched with guests. Visit their website at www.homestayny.com

Midtown
LUXURY

The Jumeirah Essex House, on the park with another entrance on 58th Street. 160 Central Park South, tel: (212) 247-0300, fax: 315-1839.

Impeccable style, excellent service, two notable restaurants. Although an older hotel it has a health spa and a business centre.

The Four Seasons, East 57th Street. Notable restaurant, 57 East 57th Street, tel: (212) 758-5700, fax: 758-5711. A huge building, palatial foyers and large rooms at this smart address on the East Side.

The Plaza, Fifth Ave, at 59th Street, tel: (212) 759-3000, fax: 759-3167. Perhaps New York's most famous hotel, facing Central Park, with the famed Oak Room. Currently part is being converted to condominums.

UN Plaza, 44th at First Avenue, tel: (212) 758-1234, fax: 702-5051.You can have an unusual experience here – play tennis and swim indoors, high up in the air and with views of the UN Building too!

The Sheraton Manhattan, 811 Seventh Avenue, tel: (212) 581-3300, fax: (212) 541-9219. Modern, huge, handy for Broadway theatres. Try Happy Hour drinks at the Tower Lounge.

Waldorf-Astoria, 301 Park Ave, tel: (212) 355-3000, fax: 759-9209. On posh Park Avenue, this hotel's old-style grandeur attracts

New York City At a Glance

the rich and famous. Elaborately gilded Art Deco style everywhere.

Most hotels are midtown, but others are popping up in revitalised districts like SoHo. Notable is the **Ritz Carlton New York Battery Park**, 2 West Street, tel: (212) 344-0800, fax: (212) 344-3804, with sweeping harbour views. In midtown, another new base for this luxury chain is **Ritz Carlton New York Central Park**, 50 Central Park South, overlooking the park; tel: (212) 308-9100, fax: (212) 207-8831. Mid-range suggestion: **Holiday Inn Wall Street**, a conventional hotel, but check low-price weekend rates through NYTAB.

MID-RANGE

The Algonquin Hotel, 59 West 44th, tel: (212) 840-6800, fax: 944-1419. Famous and popular with writers and publishers at a shrine – the Round Table met here. Alluring atmosphere, its dark-panelled lounge good for a drink or tea.

Paramount, 235 West 46th Street, tel: (212) 764-5500, fax: 575-4892. Stylishly remodelled, yet retaining a 1920s atmosphere, but rather small rooms. Near Broadway theatres. Popular with younger business people and arts types.

Wellington Hotel, 871 Seventh Ave, tel: (212) 247-3900, fax: (212) 581-1350. Good value, near to Broadway showplaces. A 1930s survivor, it also has a coffee shop and cocktail bar.

Warwick Hotel, 65 West 54th Street, tel: (212) 247-2700, fax: (212) 247-2725. On the corner of Sixth Avenue this welcoming long-established hotel is ideal for theatre visits, Fifth Avenue shops, museums. Spacious rooms and bathrooms. Popular bar and good restaurant on the ground floor. Recommended.

Suggestion: try the old-style **Sherry Netherland** for real comfort and large rooms.

BUDGET

Gramercy Park Hotel, 2 Lexington Ave, tel: (212) 475-4320, fax: 505-0535. Despite its smart townhouse aspect this small hotel is reasonable and has desirable park-facing rooms – you will also receive access to this rare green enclave.

Pickwick Arms, 230 East 51st, tel: (212) 355-0300, fax: 755-5029. This is a reasonably priced place if you want economy in midtown. There's also a roof garden and a bar available.

Stanford Hotel, 43 West 32nd, tel: (212) 563-1500,

fax: 629-0043. A small hotel that offers low prices for those on a budget and is neat and central. Well-placed for the shops at Herald Square as well as for visiting the Javits Convention Center.

Aladdin Hotel, 317 West 45th Street, tel: (212) 246-8580, fax: 246-6036. Recently renovated and centrally located, this is a bargain option for those who don't mind shared bathrooms and dormitory-style sleeping accomodation.

Vanderbilt YMCA, 224 East 47th Street, tel: (212) 755-2410. Despite the name both sexes can stop off here. This recently renovated hostel is in the heart of midtown east, has plenty of sports facilities and is close to the UN.

New York Bed and Breakfast does exist, and at a price you can stay with the genuine New Yorkers in their own homes. Try the following but be sure to check ahead of time before your arrival.

Bed and Breakfast Bureau, 330 West 42nd Street, tel: (212) 645-4555.

City Lights Bed and Breakfast Ltd, PO Box 20355, Cherokee Station, NYC, NY 10028, tel: (212) 737-7049.

New York City At a Glance

New World Bed and Break-fast, 63 South Street, NY10005, tel: (212) 675-5600.

Uptown
LUXURY
The Carlyle, 35 East 76th Street, tel: (212) 744-1600, fax: 717-4682. Notable older hotel in high Art Deco style, handy for the museums, Madison Avenue sale rooms and smart shops.

Lowell Hotel, 28 East 63rd, tel: (212) 838-1400, fax: 319-4230. If you yearn for old-world comforts (even open fires in some rooms) and are willing to pay the price for high-quality New York accommodation, this is a gem. It also has a very good restaurant.

The Mark Mandarin Oriental, 25 East 77th Street, tel: (212) 744-4300, fax: 744-2749. An elegant hotel on the Upper East Side close to the park and the Metropolitan Museum. Old-style European service and a club-like informal restaurant in the foyer.

BUDGET
International Student Center, 38 West 88th Street, it is close to Central Park, tel: (212) 787-7706. You won't meet any Americans here – it's only open to foreigners, mostly students.

It feels like old New York, a mansion on a leafy street but there are dormitory rooms inside.

Hostelling International NY, 891 Amsterdam Avenue, tel: (212) 932-2300. High on the Upper West Side this very large hostel is well looked after, offers real bargain rates, varied services and has a lovely garden.

West Side YMCA, it is just off Central Park at 5 West 63rd Street, tel: (212) 875-4100. Well-equipped if a little bit severe in style, this hostel has been very well renovated and offers bargain rooms with lots of good sport choices including an indoor running track.

Other suggestions: **The 1871 House** (Upper East Side) or the **Hotel Beacon** (Upper West Side) are top value for those who don't need to be central. Kitchen facilities, a good supermarket opposite.

Downtown
LUXURY
Millenium Hilton, 55 Church Street, tel: (212) 693-2001, fax: 571-2317. If you want to be right downtown and lapped in modern luxury, this newly refurbished hotel by the WTC site is an idea, has great views and with facilities for the business visitor.

MID-RANGE
Chelsea Hotel, 222 West 23rd Street, tel: (212) 645-8989, fax: (212) 645-1903. A rather bizarre hotel, its façade plastered with the names of the famous who have rested here, from Dylan Thomas to rock, punk and grunge stars.

Gershwin Hotel, 7 East 27th Street, tel: (212) 545-8000, fax: 684-5546. In a lively area near the new Sex Museum its red and black décor and art make it a location for fun and culture lovers. Regular performances in the Living Room.

BUDGET
Washington Square Hotel, 103 Waverly Place, tel: (212) 777-9515, fax: 979-8373. Stay right on the famous square in Greenwich Village at bargain rates in this no-frills place. Good value and all rooms recently renovated; the best ones have a park view.

Chelsea Center, two low-priced hostels, one at 313 West 29th Street, one on East 12th Street at 1st Avenue, tel: (212) 643-0214. Simple accommodation, some dormitory style, self-catering equipment.

WHERE TO EAT

The range of restaurants and eateries in this city is enormous. From local

New York City At a Glance

bakeries and hot dog stands where you can nibble on snacks as you sightsee, to chic cafés and department store restaurants, right up the top of the range eateries, there's an awe-inspiring choice. Even the cheap food places are often very good. There are many specialist places from Jewish dairy cafés to the delectable parade of vegetarian restaurants. There are quite a number of Indian places now but it seems that every country in the world is represented in this very food-conscious city with its parade of particular cuisines from Australia to Zambia. Look out for local fairs and celebrations: some of these such as Little Italy's festival are well known but look out for others. It is a lively time when whole neighbour-hoods turn out to parade and dance in the streets. During Restaurant Week, held in the last week in June, hundreds of establish-ments offer taster portions and special prix-fixe meals. Also, don't miss the dozens of Chinese restaurants around Mulberry Street. Ask for the latest recommendation in a variety of cuisines from the humble Cantonese to Pekingese and the spicy Szechwan. Foodies can go mad at the very thought of New York's incredible range

of restaurants, and if you have money to spend, there are some of the leading restaurants in the world to try. Almost all good estab-lishments will take credit cards, and New York is a city where hotel restaurants are often of a high standard too.

Midtown

LUXURY

La Côte Basque, 60 West 55th Street, tel: (212) 688-6525. A very smart restaurant serving classic French food. Famous for its evocative murals and a unique style all of its own.

The Four Seasons, 99 East 52nd Street, tel: (212) 754-9494. This is one of the sights of foodie New York, but it's not only famous as a temple to gastronomes, it is very grand and social. The place to try if you want to see smart New York at table.

The Rainbow Room, 230 Rockefeller Plaza, tel: (212) 632-5100. Now owned by Cipriani, this is a prime place to dine and dance, but it's expensive. Still, with those views from the 65th floor you should lose your head a bit. There's a nightclub too, and if you're not so hungry try the Rainbow Promenade nearby.

MID-RANGE

La Cité, 120 West 51st Street, tel: (212) 956-7100. This restaurant is large and rambling and great for good straightforward food (delicious hamburgers) and big drinks.

Pierre au Tunnel is close to the ever-busy tunnel across to Queens at 250 East 47th Street, tel: (212) 575-1220. The unusual thing about New York is the number of authentic French restaurants, and this is just like an old bistro.

The Palm, Busy and lively at 837 Second Avenue. There is another branch at 840 Second Avenue, tel: (212) 687-2953. If you feel like a steak then this crazy but fun restaurant is for you. In addition there is lobster and that very New York dish, Clams Casino.

Time, at Lafayette Place, tel: (212) 533-7000, or 2330 Broadway at 8th Street. Offers basic foods, from pizzas to tapas, as well as special dishes. Friendly and crowded, with nice bar area.

Moto, 328 West 45th Street, tel: (212) 459-9393. Maybe the best Japanese restaurant in town. Smallish menu, very friendly, good value. Only open in the evenings, closed Mondays.

New York City At a Glance

BUDGET

La Fondue, 43 West 55th
Street, tel: (212) 581-0820.
If cheese is a passion, try
this for the all-in-one
experience. They also do
beef, fish and seafood, so
you don't have to eat cheese
and afterwards try the
chocolate fondue. Low-
price, so no credit cards.

Planet Hollywood, 140 West
57th Street, tel: (212) 333-
7827. The in place for kids;
so much is going on as they
eat that the food hardly
matters. Expect to wait.

Carmine's, 200 West 44th
Street, tel: (212) 221-3800,
with a branch uptown at
2450 Broadway at 90th
Street. A noisy, friendly,
family place with a New
York-Italian atmosphere,
open till late; delicious
home-style food.

Enzo's Jazz/Whaler Bar, in
the Jolly Hotel Madison
Towers at 22 East 38th
Street, tel: (212) 802-0600. It
serves American-style snacks
and drinks before a big roar-
ing fire in this lofty place.
Entertainment is provided.
This bar is very popular
with locals.

Uptown

LUXURY

Le Cirque 2000, Palace
Hotel, 455 Madison Avenue,
tel: (212) 303-7788.

Fashionable with the well-off
and would-be famous.
Original food. Reservations
are hard to get.

MID-RANGE

Elaine's, 1703 Second
Avenue, tel: (212) 534-8114.
The sort of personality cult
place that only happens in
big cities. This is so popular
that the food, which is
eclectic, doesn't matter.

Primavera, 1578 First
Avenue, tel: (212) 861-8608.
This is a quietly-elegant
place popular with the
locals. Friendly, concerned
Italian service.

Mark's, 25 East 77th Street,
tel: (212) 879-1864.
A charming in-hotel
restaurant off the foyer,
offering food all day long
in an intimate setting.

BUDGET

American Trash, 1471 First
Avenue, tel: (212) 988-9008.
As you would suspect by the
name, this is definitely a
place for the kids and there's
usually a queue to get in.

Bistro du Nord,
1312 Madison Avenue,
tel: (212) 289-0997. You'll
find this great little French
restaurant at East 93rd Street
before reaching Spanish
Harlem. A warm welcoming
atmosphere, reasonably
priced French food.

Downtown

MID-RANGE

Katz's Delicatessen Inc, 205
East Houston, tel:
(212) 254-2246. This deli
caters mostly for older
people who enjoy the
traditional kosher food.

Cowgirl,
519 Hudson Street at 10th,
tel: (212) 633-1133. Lively
Southwestern atmosphere
and cooking. A new
favourite for the Village.

BUDGET

Koodo Sushi,
129 Front Street, tel: (212)
425-2890. A plain space
beneath the Seaport Suites
but good sushi – try a take-
out to eat on Pier 16 or 17.

Café Reggio,
119 MacDougal Street,
tel: (212) 475-9557.
Everything you expect of a
village café – dark and a
place where unusual people
gather. More for snacks than
meals. If crowded, try the
equally atmospheric Café
Dante, 79 MacDougal, tel:
(212) 982-5275.

Dean and Deluca Café,
121 Prince Street, tel: (212)
226-6800. Spin-off from the
renowned groceries (there's
a big one at the roadway
corner) in SoHo. This is a
good place to pop in and
enjoy a quick snack or have
a cup of coffee.

New York City At a Glance

Fedora's,
239 West 4th Street,
tel: (212) 242-9691.
This restaurant has been a
village landmark for more
than 50 years. Big drinks,
cheap eats, a bit tatty but
charming Fedora is still
hostess here.

Beyond Manhattan
LUXURY
River Café,
1 Water Street, Brooklyn
Heights, tel: (212) (718) 522-
5200. Just to show that not all
of the expensive places are
situated in Manhattan itself,
this smart spot cashes in
on the view from Brooklyn –
it is located near the famous
landmark Brooklyn Bridge
where the one-time barge
is moored.

Water's Edge,
44th Drive, Long Island City,
tel: (212) (718) 482-0033.
Another smart place
that takes advantage
of Manhattan views. This
seafood restaurant is on
the city edge of Long Island
in Queens, and formal.

MID-RANGE
Henry's End, 44 Henry
Street, Brooklyn, tel: (718)
834-1776. Good value and
unusual cuisine here – such
as kangaroo and elk.

Odessa, 1113 Brighton
Beach Avenue, tel: (718)
332-3223. So you want to

try the new Russia? Come to
Brighton Beach in Brooklyn
and try the parade of dishes
and vodka, and dancing too.

BUDGET
Pastrami King, 124-24
Queens Blvd, tel: (718)
263-1717. New Yorkers
get sentimental about where
to get good salt beef, or
pastrami, and this is a real
'deli' in Queens.

SHOPPING

A place to stretch your legs,
in **department stores**, in
speciality stores of every
kind, in **markets** and even
galleries. Whatever you
require, however much you
have to spend, shoppers can
find heaven here, and the city
is also a great fashion centre.
In many countries the dollar
exchange rate is good and the
amounts of cash you can
bring in are considerable. In
addition almost every place
in New York takes plastic, but
check which credit cards are
available before you buy.
There are great bargains to be
found here, particularly in
clothes, household goods,
gadgets, electrical and
computer products, linens,
books and CDs. You can find
top labels on sale, (January
and other sales are popular
times, especially along West
34th Street) or go slumming
and sift through stuff on
Orchard Street stalls. Even
thrift shops in the smart areas

can produce good buys and
offer fascinating browsing.
Try **Greenmarket** in Union
Square for fruit, bread and
vegetables. Invaluable for
self-caterers.

Bookshops are open late and
often provide a social hub for
like-minded folk, not only for
browsers but in their self-
contained coffee shops and
sitting areas. Ursus Books, 132
West 21st Street, tel: (212) 627
5370 – or at the Carlyle Hotel
– are recommended for art
books and bargains.

Main areas for general
shopping are Fifth Avenue
from 34th up to 59th, West
34th Street and the vast shopping malls out of the centre.
These often have branches
of top Fifth Avenue shops
such as **Saks**, **Bergdorf
Goodman** and **Lord and
Taylor** as part of the complex.
FAO Schwarz is a wonderland of toys for kids at 58th
Street. Individual stores in
Manhattan, not in main-
stream areas, include smart
Bloomingdale's, the new
Abraham and Strauss on
A & S Plaza, Sixth Avenue
and 33rd, and malls such as
Century Plaza. On newly
smart Sixth Avenue below
23rd Street you can shop at
Filene's, and next door at
18th Street **Old Navy** stocks
trendy sports and casual wear.

Discount stores line Lower
Broadway, and even the
Financial District has lures.
Here you can find Century 21

New York City At a Glance

Discounts (22 Cortlandt Street) and bargains at J and R Music and Computer World (31 Park Row). For discount fashion and much more try Daffy's (135 East 57th Street, and five other branches).

Don't overlook **museum shops** – big ones at the Metropolitan and Museum of Modern Art, or whole shopping sections in attractions such as the **South Street Seaport**. If you want to shop but don't have the time, department stores will do it for you with your own **personal shopper** who will discuss your needs and then select items or guide you to specific departments.

If you don't care for big stores, **Madison Avenue** from 42nd Street up has a galaxy of small stylish shops and **East 57th Street** a parade of expensive galleries and boutiques.

Antique shops are all over the Upper East Side with markets like the **Place des Antiquaries** on East 57th, the **Arts and Antique Center** at Second Avenue and East 56th and along Third Avenue. At the other end of the scale cheap goods can be found along 14th Street, Canal Street, Broadway and in parts of the Lower East Side. Even once exclusive Fifth Avenue in the 40s and 50s has cheap emporiums selling jewellery, carpets and decorative items.

Food shops abound on main avenues like Second, Third and Upper Broadway, but check that foodstuffs can be imported before you leave home. Also be sure that with electrical and software goods you can use them beyond the US. (Bridge Kitchenware at 214 East 52nd Street is helpful here.) You may need converters or adaptors. Be aware that a sizable sales tax is added to purchases.

TOURS AND EXCURSIONS

From **coach tours** to **walks**, from **helicopter flights** to **cruises** around the harbour, there are lots of possibilities. It's a good idea to check with tourist offices for local trips and ideas. Try **Circle Lines** and **New York Waterway** for exploratory trips. Other craft cruise the harbour from the **South Street Seaport** base, or you can even charter your own. The classic harbour cruise is still the one on the Staten Island Ferry and back, but there are also frequent day services out to Liberty and Ellis Islands and the sometimes open Governor's Island. Several companies offer Harlem tours with visits to Gospel churches and a typical soul food meal. Beyond New York try **Greyhound** coach lines or you can rent private cars to be driven out to Connecticut, New Jersey, Long Island and other parts

of New York State.
Bicycling
Rent bikes in Central Park at the **Loeb Boathouse**, tel: (212) 517-2233. Other rental places are listed in the commercial section of the NY phone books. Or try popular bike-powered rickshaws.
Gray Line of New York
A standard day-long hop-on, hop-off tour or a quick 2-hour introduction is available from 900 Eighth Avenue, for schedules tel: (212) 445-0848 and (toll free) 800 669 0051.
Shortline Bus Tours
All day or a few hours, a variety available, schedules from 166 West 46th Street, tel: (toll free) 800 631 8405.
Harlem Tours
Harlem Spirituals Inc, 1457, 1697 Broadway, tel: (212) 757-0425 and **Harlem Heritage**, tel: (212) 280-788. For other ideas and details of Limo Tours, *see* page 97.
Helicopter Tours
Try Liberty Helicopter, West 30th Street and 12th Avenue, tel: (212) 967-6464 for a bird's-eye view. Also Pier 6, Whitehall Street, tel: (212) 487-4777.
Ponycabs
For a romantic carriage trot around Manhattan or the park, 517 Broome Street, tel: (212) 773-8844.
Walking Tours
Offered by several organizations around the city. Ask

New York City At a Glance

at the information offices for they are often geared to specific areas or interests such as architecture, museums, the community and the arts.

In such a big city you ought to be prepared. New Yorkers are friendly enough, but on the streets they don't always like to talk to strangers, even if they are tourists, so asking questions can be a problem. **Big Apple Greeters:** individual volunteers who offer an insider's point of view of New York, tel: (212) 669-2896. **Entertainment Information**, a free service updated daily to inform you what's on in New York, 24-hour service, tel: 360-3333. Try also **New York City Onstage** for all arts events, 24 hours, tel: (212) 768-1818. Information is also available at the new Embassy Theatre centre (*see* below). **Theater Tkts** is a booth selling half-price theatre tickets on Times Square, also at Front and John streets at the South Street Seaport. Queue for day of performance tickets for events on and off Broadway. **Post Office:** scattered around the city, in each zipcode section, the main one is at Eighth Avenue and 33rd Street. **NYC & Company**, 810 Seventh Avenue at 52/53 Streets, tel: (212) 884-2000, www.nycvisit.com Useful provider of advice and infor-

mation as well as leaflets, maps, lists of tour operators, etc. For free information and brochures (ask for the *Official NYC Guide*, a pocket-sized quarterly compendium), visit one of the tourist offices situated in the following places: Lobby of the Embassy Theater, 47th and Broadway; Bloomingdale's, Third Avenue; Macy's, 34th Street; Grand Central Terminal; Kennedy Airport. Open every day 09:00–17:00. To pick up a free map, guide, or discount coupon book, call NYTAB, tel: (212) 267 1922. **Time:** to find out the time, tel: (212) 976-1616. **Weather:** information on television or in newspapers or tel: (607) 721-1597.

It may not be advertised as such in brochures and tourist information, but as a city, New York also sells sex. It is available here even though the city authorities continually attempt to 'clean it up'. There's even a museum of sex at Fifth

Avenue and East 27th Street – opened in 2003, it's quite a lure. Prostitutes used to swarm in the theatre district – now cleaned up – and they have moved to Lower Manhattan and the lorry parks in Brooklyn. The crack sellers still crouch in alleys off Eighth Avenue.

Exotically dressed, some of the 'girls' are transvestites. Boys are also available along some avenues and in a number of East and West Side bars; at the Gaiety Club on West 46th Street, naked studs strip and show. For voyeurs there are sex-cinemas (along midtown Eighth Avenue) with hard-core films. There are live sex shows too, even on Broadway. In New York anything goes, and liberal laws means that if someone wants it, you can find it here. But take care if you walk or drive through some neighbourhoods as theft and sometimes violence are not uncommon. And it should go without saying, if you do participate take condoms: safe sex is *de rigueur*.

NEW YORK CITY	J	F	M	A	M	J	J	A	S	O	N	D
AVERAGE TEMP. °C	0	1	5	11	17	22	25	24	20	15	8	2
AVERAGE TEMP. °F	32	33	41	52	62	71	77	75	68	58	47	36
Hours of sun daily	2	3	4	6	7	8	9	8	7	4	3	2
Days of rainfall	12	10	12	11	11	10	12	10	9	9	9	10
RAINFALL mm	94	97	91	81	81	84	107	109	86	89	76	91
RAINFALL in	4	4	4	3.5	3.5	3.5	4	4	3.5	3.5	3	4

Travel Tips

Tourist Information

As cutbacks cause the closure of government agencies, the private sector is taking over. The New York Travel Advisory Bureau's visitor kit (*see* panel page 12) offers maps, discount and information; obtainable in the UK, tel: 0906 11 22 668. Calls cost about £4, covering shipping of 2 kits by Global Priority Mail. Try your travel agent or the NYC and Company (*see* page 121 for contact details). In some countries the State of New York may be represented in its own right.

Entry Requirements

You will need a valid passport, but citizens of 27 countries no longer need a visa to enter, although you can apply for one and then don't need to worry about possible delays on entering. If you have any queries about passports etc contact your local **US Embassy Visa Division** before making plans. Non US residents fill in two forms on arrival and queues form before booths as each entrant is interviewed at the entry point, which takes time.

Customs

Immigration and custom formalities at most airports are now swift and efficient. At some airports sniffer dogs are used to check baggage and they will also indicate if you are carrying fresh fruit, vegetable, dairy or meat products. Check beforehand what is not allowed for importation. There are certain duty free allowances to every visitor and US resident so find out before you buy.

Health Requirements

No inoculation certificates are needed, unless you have recently been in an area with an epidemic of cholera, yellow fever, or other contagious sickness. You may be interviewed if you have recently visited a farm in the country you are coming from. If you are taking medication involving drugs, it is wise to have a doctor's letter as proof that you are not bringing in illicit substances. Remember there is very little assistance for health problems in the USA, and treatment is very costly, so along with insurance for bag-

gage, theft or trip-cancellation costs you should most definitely take out comprehensive medical insurance for the period of your visit.

Getting There

By Air: The airports are within easy reach of the city. There are coach connections to **Grand Central** and the **Port Authority (PA)** from **Kennedy** and **LaGuardia**, to the PA from **Newark**. The morning and evening rush hours can lengthen the time taken considerably. There are car rental offices and usually numerous taxis on hand. There is now a fixed taxi fare from JFK to Manhattan – around $45 plus tolls and tip. There are few services between midnight and 06:00.

By Rail: The bargain from Kennedy to Midtown Manhattan is the subway which is less than an hour's duration and is a flat fare. Take the AirTrain to the subway station on the airport perimeter (Howard Beach / JFK) and then the fast A train which goes to express stops on the Eighth Avenue line in

Manhattan. Some hotels provide courtesy coaches and there are free shuttle bus services for getting to the various airport terminals. In the planning stages are a Monorail connection to JFK, and the new Penn Station to Newark AP is in operation.

By Road: Drive on the right. Roads into Manhattan are major highways, and well marked. Cars pay tolls at most entry points. In the city, roads can be badly deformed and pot-holed: drive carefully. Traffic lights are synchronized along main avenues. Drivers need to carry their licenses and for self-drive cars, full insurance should definitely be considered.

What to Pack

Dress is generally informal, although if you plan to play high stakes and live the smart life of Manhattan you will need fashionable wear, formal gear for good restaurants, including jackets and ties for men and no jeans. Good and comfortable footwear is important, but they don't have to be unattractive, just well broken in. It can be very cold in winter, so pack warm clothes and take gloves and scarves and you may need to get galoshes if it is snowing. This can be a place of extremes, and though New York streets are cleaned quickly, as a rule pavements can be very messy. Take a folding umbrella and rainwear. It is cool and temperate in the short spring and the longer fall, but it can get very hot and

---

frightfully humid in summer when shorts, blouses or lightweight shirts are necessary. For summer cocktail parties or dinners, however, take lightweight formal wear.

Money Matters

The American dollar (a buck) is the unit and each dollar is divided into 100 cents. Coins are issued in denominations of 1c (called a cent or sometimes a penny) 5c (a nickel), 10c (a dime), 25c (a quarter) 50c and a dollar (dollar coins arc not common except in some western states). Notes (paper money) are available in denominations of $1, $2 (rare) $5, $10, $20, $50, $100, $500 and up. Designs of notes are not too different and as the basic colour is the same green you may need to check carefully when paying in cash. Paper money and coins have hardly changed at all except for metal content, which is a bonus as cash or coinage from previous trips will still be legal

---

tender. The American dollar has fallen against many currencies over the past decade but has stabilized recently.

Currency Exchange: Most currencies are easily exchanged for dollars, and there are no restrictions except that you may not bring more than $10,000 in cash into the USA without making a declaration to Customs. You can take in cash below this limit, or dollar traveller's cheques and exchange money at airport and station booths or at machines taking credit or some bank cards.

Banks: There are some national banks in the USA, and many private ones. Open 09:00 to 15:00. Monday–Friday. Cash machines taking most credit and bank cards are everywhere. Banks will need some form of identification for business other than exchanging cash, such as when changing traveller's cheques. Take a photo ID or a passport. Hotels will change money, though their rates won't necessarily be advantageous. Accredited dealers and travel agents have outlets in main centres, but it's wise to compare exchange rates, especially if cashing large amounts of money.

Credit Cards: The major ones (Visa, Access, American Express, Diners, Delta and Mastercard) are accepted everywhere for many transactions from shopping to petrol. You can also utilize them to get cash. Practically all hotels, restaurants, travel agents and hire companies accept plastic. It is wise however, to take out an insurance policy against theft on all your credit cards.

Tipping: Regardless of the quality of service (or lack of it) most people add 15% to restaurant and bar bills, taxi-fares and services from hotel room staff. Beware the wrath of some drivers, porters or waiters untipped in certain restaurants. Porters often have a fixed rate. When checking out remember there will be City and State taxes added to your bill (also on shopping and for meals).

Gambling: You can gamble in many ways in New York. Popular are horse and surrey racing, results of boxing or wrestling matches and other sports.

Accommodation

A vast range of prices from the most luxurious and expensive hotels in the world to simple motels on the West Side or even bed-and-breakfasts. And for students and the budget-minded there are plain down-to-earth dormitory hostels. You can book ahead using services or there are booking facilities for hotels at the airports and stations.

Eating Out

You are spoiled for choice in New York. Every kind of food is available from the best of the Parisian style and New York cooking to soul food. Many snack bars offer sand-wiches – some New York favourites such as pastrami salt beef and of course, big ham-burgers are bargains. Pretzels and bagels are typical snacks. Steak houses offer grilled meats and salads at competi-tion prices. Local restaurants have special offers, big sand-wiches and rich desserts.

Transport

New York has a well-developed, reasonable public transport system. The subway is extensive, covering four boroughs, and operates on a flat fare system. There's also the Staten Island Railway, not part of the subway system. Bus services on main avenue and cross streets at flat fare, sometimes transfers to and from subways are possible. New York is a terminus for many airlines and trains. Coaches and trains provide airport connections to Grand Central Terminal and the Port Authority.

Women Travellers: There are many precautions that need to be considered in a city like New York where a solitary woman can feel unsafe in some areas. Though less a problem over the past decade, it's important to appear confi-dent and alert, and you can be prepared by going to informa-tion offices and asking about safety in the city.

Business Hours

Americans seem to work longer and longer hours, and New York is no exception with the bizarre 'power break-fasts' starting as early as 06:30. Business, however, doesn't get geared up at most offices until 08:30 or 09:00 and goes on often without lunch breaks to 17:30 or 18:00, Monday–Friday. Most banks have 24 hour automatic cash machines (you may need to swipe a bank or credit card to enter the space). Shops and supermarkets stay open later on most evenings (Thursday shopping to 21:00 at depart-ment stores) and are also open on Sundays. Some foodstores serve customers past midnight. Fruit, veg and food stalls, especially along the lower East Side avenues, are open all night as are some cafés and snack bars, which even if they are not 24-hour operations,

CONVERSION CHART		
FROM	**TO**	**MULTIPLY BY**
Millimetres	Inches	0.0394
Metres	Yards	1.0936
Metres	Feet	3.281
Kilometres	Miles	0.6214
Square Kilometres	Square miles	0.386
Hectares	Acres	2.471
Litres	Pints	1.760
Kilograms	Pounds	2.205
Tonnes	Tons	0.984
To convert Celsius to Fahrenheit: x 9 ÷ 5 + 32		

start early and close late. Many bars of which there is a great variety in New York, are open all day and often only close for a couple of hours at night, usually from 04:00–06:00 to clean up. Big hotels will have round the clock reception and room service facilities.

Time Difference

New York is five hours behind GMT, and puts its clocks forward for one hour during summer time.

Communications

Telecommunications: Public telephones in the city are run by several companies. Numbers consist of a three-digit code and seven-digit numbers. Manhattan numbers are prefixed either 212 or 646 – even local calls must be prefixed with theit three-digit code. For all calls beyond Manhattan you need to add 1 before the ten digits. 800 calls are toll-free numbers, 900 numbers are definitely not, and they can be costly. Directory assistance for local calls is 411, for long distance dial 555 1212 prefixing with the usual 1 and the area code. You can make person-to-person or collect calls or pay with coins, using public phones, but as this can mean a large handful of loose change for calls made through the operator from public phones it's best to buy a telephone card, or use any one of several credit cards.
Help Lines: There are a number of help telephone lines to

assist you. **The Yellow Pages** list agencies and counselling aids.
Postal services: Post offices are based at each zip code area of the city, with the main one at 34th Street and 8th Avenue being **New York 10001**. (The whole country has five digit codes, and to speed delivery sometimes there is an additional four digit number attached). Postage varies from postcards to local mail and if you need special stamps there is some-times a particular counter. All services are offered plus copying and fax in most offices. If you require to receive mail tell correspon-dents to send letters allowing plenty of delivery time, c/o General Delivery at New York City, NY addressed to the specific zip code of the office at which you wish to pick up mail. Post offices are open from 08:00–17:00 and from 08:00 to midday on Saturdays. Closed on all public holidays.

Electricity

The system uses 110–120 volts 60 cycles in the USA. The plugs are two-pin, so when buying a necessary current converter ensure it will work in the US.

Weights and Measures

The USA consistently refuses to go metric, unlike Canada, and abides by the old British system of measuring in feet, yards and miles. For weights they use pounds and ounces and the regular gallon (not

the imperial) and pints for liquids. People have little idea of metric equivalents so if buying shoes, clothes or fab-rics you may need to convert. Temperatures are measured in **Fahrenheit**.

Health Precautions

Do not even think of going to New York without taking adequate medical insurance. Buy it for the trip, as part of a regular insurance policy, or at the last minute where it can be purchased at some airports. It could cost a fortune for anyone unlucky enough to fall ill here without coverage, for though hospitals are right up to date they are very costly places to stay in. There are some free hospitals ('charity' ones) but they are crowded and overworked and often understaffed, otherwise all hospitals are private. You can see a general practitioner or in an emergency go direct to a casualty ward. They will usually want proof that you can pay your bill before offering services (often a recognized credit card imprint suffices). However, they **must** treat you regardless of this pressure.

Health Services

Very minimal unless you are prepared to pay substantially. New York has the finest hospitals and clinics, but you'll need a credit card. It's imperative to take out health insurance for a visit here. Note NYTAB offers a UK or Euro policy.

Personal Safety

It's sensible not to look like a tourist. Try and avoid the obvious clothes and appendages such as camera bags. And most importantly for women, conceal or don't wear jewellery. Keep your wallet or purse in one pocket and have ready money in another, or wear one of those unattractive yet useful money belts. Take only what you need, maybe concealing an extra note somewhere about your person, although muggers have been known to check inside shoes. Carry at least one, preferably two, forms of identification. On the streets, walk as if you know where you are going, dawdling and too much 'rubber-necking' can mark you out. Avoid poor and dangerous areas, and at night don't walk in parks. Don't get caught up with con artists – there are lots of them in the city, operating all sorts of

tricks. Hustlers are common in certain areas such as the **Pennsylvania Station**. Ask directions from policemen or doormen or BIDs, or go into shops or cafés. Never leave anything that looks valuable and that can be seen in a car. If you are travelling at night it's preferable to use surface transport but if there is no bus, then stay near subway token booths until the train arrives. Some stations will have a posse of the so-called **Guardian Angels** on hand in their red berets to ensure safety. For more info visit www.guardianangels.org Late at night the safest form of transport is a taxi.

Senior Citizens: Always ask if there are concessions. If you are taking medication, or may need assistance, remember to keep a note to that effect on your person in order to pass on the information to a helper.

Emergencies

Embassies and Consulates: New York has a large representation of consulates, listed in the telephone book. If you require assistance from your embassy, you may need to contact the capital, Washington. There are UN missions from most countries based in New York.

Etiquette

New Yorkers are not truly Americans – much as Berliners are not German. New York is a state of mind as well as a great city. The residents are proud of being New Yorkers and don't care for undue criti-

cism from anybody. Note for puffers: no smoking is allowed in bars, restaurants, offices or public buildings.

Language

English is spoken everywhere in the USA, but in some neighbourhoods you will still hear a European tongue or even Yiddish. Almost everyone understands and speaks English, but in some cities, notably New York and Miami, **Spanish** is very much a major second language. The influx of Mexicans has made Spanish a second language in LA, but it is mostly due to the Puerto Rican influx in NY City that large numbers of the population hardly use English at all.The arrival of new Caribbean and South American settlers has brought French and Portuguese into the mix. You might have a French-speaking Haitian as a cab driver!

GOOD READING

While you are in New York City, don't forget to get hold of a copy of *The New York Times* or *Village Voice* for news and information on current events. There are also several magazines, such as *The New Yorker,* the *New York Magazine* and *Time Out Magazine,* which are very interesting and filled with helpful information.
• Morrone, Francis, *The Architectural Guidebook to New York City* (Gibbs-Smith).
• Alleman, Richard, *The Movie Lover's Guide to New York* (Harper & Row).

INDEX

accommodation 114, 115, 116, 124
Aids Memorial **98**
Albany 6, 111
Algonquin Indians 9, 11, 14
Algonquin Hotel 23
Alice Tully Hall 91
Alphabet City **41**
Amagansett 5, 107
American Civil War 14, 15
American Folk Art Museum 76
American Football 26
American Museum of Natural History 87, 89, 92
Apollo Theater 24, 96
Aqueduct Race Track 103
Art Deco 23, **24**, 25, 35, 67, 71, 72, 75, 83, 93
Astor Place 52
Atlantic City **109**
Audubon Terrace 96
Aunt Len's Doll and Toy Museum 96
Avenue of the Arts 10
Avery Fisher Hall 24, 91

Balanchine, George 24
Bank of Manhattan 62
Barnard College 95, 98
Bartholdi, Frédéric 32
baseball **26**
basketball 26
Battery, The 9, 31, 32, 34, 37
Bayard Building 42
Bear Mountain 111
Belvedere Castle 82
Bethesda Fountain 82
Bloomingdale's 14, 68, **84**
Boricua College 96
Boss Tweed 12
Bowery, The 39, 42, 44, 45
Brighton Beach 107
British Museum 85
Broadway 9, 10, 22, 23, 25, 35, 44, 45, 47, 50, 53, 55, 60, 61, 65, 74, 89, 91
Bronx, The 5, 7, 26
Bronx Zoo 7, 87, **104**
Brooklyn 5, 7, 10, 26, 102, 103
Brooklyn Battery Tunnel 102
Brooklyn Botanical Garden 103
Brooklyn Bridge 14, 15, **37**
Brooklyn Heights 32, 102
buskers **20**
Butler Library 98

Canal Street 39, 40, 53, 56
Cape May 109
Caribbean Islands 39
Carnegie Hall 15, **24**, 72
Castle Clinton 32
Castro, Fidel 96
Cathedral of St John the Divine 14, 21, 95, 98
Cather, Willa 23
Catskill Mountains 111
Central Park 5, 6, 7, 8, 10, 14, 15, 20, 21, 26, **81**, 82, 83, 87, **92**
Chagall 76, 85
Chanin Building 65, 72
Charles II 13
Chelsea 10, 25, 59, 62
Chelsea Hotel 23, 59, **62**
Children's Museum of Manhattan 93, 104
Chinatown 28, 36, **39**, 42, **43**, **44**
Chinese New Year 40
Christopher Street **49**, 51, 52, 53
Chrysler building **16**, 25, 62, 65, 71
Church of the Incarnation 72
City Hall 36
Civic Center 31, 36
climate 7, 113, 121
Cloisters, The 95, 99
Colonnade, The 46
Columbia University 12, 95, 98
Columbus Circle 93
Columbus Day Parade 21
Connecticut 101, 110
Cooper, Peter 46
Cooper Union 39, 45, 46
Cotton Club 96, 97
Coward, Noël 16
Cuba 21, 28
Cushman Row 62
customs 122

Daily News Building 72
Dakota Apartments 92
De Kooning 87
Delacorte Theater 83

Dinkins, Mayor 18
Dutch West Indies Company 11
Dutch settlers 9, 11, 12, 14, 31, 35

East Houston Street 39, 41
East River 6, 7
East Village 25, **45**
Easthampton 5
eating out 116, 117, 118, 119, 124
Eighth Avenue 27
El Barrio 96, 97
Ellis Island 14, 15, 31, 32, 33
Empire State Building 5, 10, 14, 16, 18, 25, 59, 62, **65**
Erie Canal 13, 14

FAO Schwarz 73
Federal Hall National Monument 35
Federal Reserve Bank 35
Fifth Avenue 5, 9, 10, 50, 52, 61, 63, 65, 72, 73, 74, 78, 81, **83**, 85, 90, 97, 99
Financial District 9, 13, 17, 25, 28, 31, 36, 56
Finger Lakes 111
Fire Island 5, 106, 107
Flatiron Building 59, 61, 62
Ford Foundation 72
Fordham University 89
Fort Tryon Park 95, 99
Fort Washington Park 99
Fort Williams 32
Four Seasons Restaurant 27, 77
Fraunces Tavern 31, 34
Frick Collection 74, 81, 86
Fuller Building 59, 77
Fulton Fish Market 37

Garment District 65, 66
General Electric Building 77
George Washington Bridge 95, 108
Giants' Stadium 26
Giuliani, Mayor 18
Goethe–Institut 84
Grace Church 47
Gramercy Park 59, 62, **63**
Grand Central Station 25, 65, **71**, 81
Great Depression 14, 16,

17, 67
Greenwich Village 5, 9, 10, 13, 19, 22, 45, 49, 51, 54
Guggenheim Museum 85
Gulf War 18

Hamilton Grange 96
Hamptons, The 107
Harlem 7, 10, 13, 14, 19, **95**, 96
Harlem Third World Trade Center 96
Hartford 110
Harvard Club 63
Haughwort Building 55
Hayden Planetarium 87, 89, 92
Hispanics 20, 21, 39
history 11–17
Holliday, Billy 97
hotels 114, 115, 116
Houston Street 40, 50
Hudson River 5, 6, 14, 16, 50, **53**, 99, **111**
Hudson, Henry 14
Hyde Park 111

immigrants 14, 15, 20, 33
International Center of Photography 84
International Wildlife Conservation Center 8

Jacob K Javits Conference Center 68
Jacques Marchais Center of Tibetan Art 105
James, Henry 23, 52
Jefferson Market Courthouse 52, 53
Jewish Lower East Side 39
Jewish Museum 84
Judson Memorial Church 52
Juilliard School 24, 89
Jumeirah Essex House 25, 27, 73

Kennedy Airport 102, 103
Kennedy, John F **18**
King, Martin Luther 18
Knickerbockers 26
Koch, Ed 15, 18

Lafayette Place 46
Lafayette Street 39
LaGuardia Airport 103
LaGuardia, Fiorello 14, 16, 18
Lake Champlain 111

Lambertville 109
Lever Building 17
Lexington Avenue 63
Lincoln Center 5, 14, 17, 24, 53, 89, 90, **91**
Lind, Jenny 32
Litchfield **110**
Little Italy 22, 28, 39, 42, 43
Little Red Lighthouse‟ **99**
Little Russia 107
Long Island 5, 7, 27, 101, **106**, 107, 109
Lord and Taylor's 73
Lower East Side 13, 15, 35, 40, 41, 42, 43, 45

MacDougal Street 51
Macy's 65, **68**, 69
Madison Avenue 73, 83
Madison Square Garden 24, 25, 26, 59, 61, 67
Manhattan 5, 6, 7, 9, 13, 14, 17, 19, 29, 31, 32, 33, 34, 65, 72
Manhattan Antique Center 73
Marble Collegiate Church 72
Mark Hotel 27
Metropolitan Museum of Art 15, **22**, 81, 83, 85, **86**
Metropolitan Opera House 90, **91**
Midtown 5, 10, 13, 19, 22, 25, 59, 63, 65, 91
Millennium Hotel 27
Mills Mansion 111
Moore, Clement 62
More, Thomas **87**
Morningside Park 95, 98
Mott Street 44
Mulberry Street 43
Murray Hill 70
Museo del Barrio 84, 97
Museum of American Constitutional Government 34
Museum of Chinese in the Americas 45
Museum of Jewish Heritage 34
Museum of Modern Art 22, 65, **76**
Museum of the American Indian 34
Museum of the City of New York 84

National Academy of Design 84

New Amsterdam 11, 12
New England 110
New Haven 110
New Hope 109
New Jersey 5, 26, 42, 53, 56, 101, 108
New London 110
New York Aquarium 32, 103, 107
New York Botanical Gardens 7, 104
New York Historical Society 93
New York Public Library 15, 65, **69**
New York State Theater 24, 91
New York Stock Exchange 35
New York University 52
Newhouse Center 104
Newport 110
Nureyev, Rudolf 92

Off-Broadway 23, 50
O'Keeffe 87
Old Colony Club 63
Old Docks, The 37, 54
Old Merchant's House 46
Olmsted, Frederick Law 82, 93, 99
O'Neill, Eugene 110
One Wall Street 35
Orchard Street 39, **41**
Oyster Bar 27

Pan Am Building 72
Paramount Hotel 27
Park Avenue 65, 83
Parker, Charlie 97
Pennsylvania Station 25, 67, 106
Picasso 76, 85
Pierpont Morgan Library 65, 70
Place des Antiquaires 73
Plaza 73, 78
Poe, Edgar Allan 50
Pollock 87
Princeton 101, 108
Prohibition 14, 96
Puck Building 42

Quakers 11, 103
Queens 5, 7, 102, 103

Radio City Music Hall **23**, 25, **75**
restaurants 116–119
Rhode Island 110
Richmond 5, **105**

Riverside Park 89, 93
Riverside Church **89**
Rockefeller Center 7, 16, 25, 65, 74, 75, 78

São Paulo 20
St Mark's in the Bowery 45
St Mark's Place **9**, 47
St Patrick's Cathedral 21, 74, **79**
St Paul's Chapel 35
Saks 73
San Francisco 22, 28, 40, 42, 43
Schermerhorn Row 37
Seagram Building 5, 17, 77
Seaport Liberty Cruise 37
Shea Stadium 24, 26, 103
shopping 119
Siegal-Cooper 63
slavery 14, 95
Smithsonian Institute 34
Snug Harbour 104, 105
SoHo 5, 10, 22, 49, **54**, 57
South Street Seaport 31, **36**, **111**
Spanish Harlem 19, 81, 95
Spanish Museum 97
Staten Island 5, 7, 32, 33, 101, 105
Staten Island Ferry 31, 33, 55
Statue of Liberty 5, 14, 15, **31**, 32, 33
Stock Market Crash 14
Stonecutting Yard 98
Stonewall Riots 53
Strand Book Store 52, 90
Striver's Row 96
Stuyvesant, Peter **11**, 14, 45, 103
Symphony Space 93

Tammany Hall 12
TKTS (Theater tickets) Booth 23, **25**, 74
Temple Emmanu-El 87
Theater District 13, 27
Theodore Roosevelt's Birthplace 87
Theological Seminary 62
Tiffany's **73**
Times Square 23, 65, **74**
Tompkins Square Park 47
tourist information centres 121, 122
tours 120, 121
transport 113, 114
travel tips 122–126
Triangle Shirtwaist

Factory 15
TriBeCa 10, 22, 49, 56, 57
Trinity Church 35
Trump Tower **9**, 78
Twain, Mark 110
Tweed Courthouse 36

Union Square 59, 60, 61
United Nations Building **17**, **70**
United States Custom House 34
University Club 63
Upper Broadway 23
Upper East Side 10, 19, 62, 81
Upper West Side 10, 13, 22, 23, 89, 90

Van Cortland House Museum 104
Vanderbilt Mansion 111
Van Gogh 85
Vaux, Calvert 82
Vermeer 86
Verrazano, Giovanni de 14
Victory Theater 15
Vivian Beaumont Theater 91

Waldorf-Astoria 25, **78**
Walker, Jimmy 16
Wall Street 9, 16, 35
War of Independence 12, 14, 34, 99
Warhol, Andy 87
Washington, George **12**, 34, 35, 52, 104
Washington Heights 10, 95, 98–99
Washington Square 49, **52**, 53,
West Point Military Academy 111
Wharton, Edith 23
Whitney Museum 34, 81, 87
Winter Garden 34
Woolworth Building 10
World Financial Center 34
World Trade Center 14, **19**, 31, 34, 35, 62
World Trade Towers 17
Wright, Frank Lloyd 85
Wright, Wilbur 14

Yale 110
Yiddish 21

Zabar's 93